FAMILY WALKS
IN THE WHITE PEAK

Norman Taylor

Scarthin Books, Cromford, Derbyshire   1991

A

FAMILY WALKS
IN THE WHITE PEAK
For Sue, Matthew and Sam

———————

THE COUNTRY CODE
Guard against all risk of fire
Fasten all gates
Keep dogs under proper control
Keep to paths across farm land
Avoid damaging fences, hedges and walls
Leave no litter
Safeguard water supplies
Protect wildlife, wild plants and trees
Go carefully on country roads
Respect the life of the countryside

———————

Published by Scarthin Books, Cromford, Derbyshire 1985

Reprinted 1985. Revised 1987. Revised 1991.

Phototypesetting, printing by Higham Press Ltd., Shirland, Derbyshire

ISBN 0 907758 09 6

WOLFSCOTE DALE   Route 4

Preface

Over the past 13 years, partly in the context of my job as a teacher, and partly out of my own need to escape to the countryside, I have spent many hours walking, climbing and pottering about in the Peak National Park. Two and a half years ago, when my partner and I became a family of three, countryside pursuits took on a somewhat different dimension, as did the contents of the rucksack. At that time, where we chose to walk and potter about was of little interest to the baby, who was more or less content in his back-carrier. But little ones grow. They want to walk - a little bit -and throw stones and sticks into streams - a lot. Thus, it became obvious that one or two compromises would have to be made for the family outings. Namely, short but interesting round walks, at some point along which it would be possible to organize a motorised rescue operation. Since no existing walkers' guides catered for this sort of complicated arrangement and, at the same time, fulfilled the needs of all concerned, a fresh look at the map was called for, to work out suitable itineraries. This, and a suggestion from a friend that I should disseminate this information to other needy parents, provided the spark which resulted in this guide.

Indeed, a number of friends and acquaintances have helped me in one way or another to produce this little book, and I am deeply indebted to them for their involvement and encouragement.

I would like to thank two people especially, Gez Boothby and his collaborator Wendy Brown, who rigorously checked out the walks and were forthcoming in their criticism, advice, and suggestions during the preparation of the guide. Ken and Elaine Wrigley and their children, Andrew and Charlotte, sampled some of the walks and provided me with a valuable yardstick, and it was Ken who initially prompted me to write a guide. I would like to thank my publishers, Dave Mitchell and George Power, for their critical input, their enthusiasm and their willingness to venture into a very competitive area. I am also grateful to staff and children at Broad Elms School, who were willing guinea-pigs in this all-weather experiment. Graeme Johnson I must thank for his continual supply of film and the long loan of various specialized equipment. To Sue, my wife, I owe a great deal, both for her encouragement and also because she created the 'space' for me to allow a hobby to become a time-consuming preoccupation. In addition, she accompanied me on a number of trial runs carrying a rucksack full of the requisites of a tiny tot, himself usually riding on his Dad's back in a child-carrier. And finally, I am deeply grateful to my mother and father, who opened my eyes to the treasures of the countryside.   N.T.

CONTENTS

MAP OF THE AREA

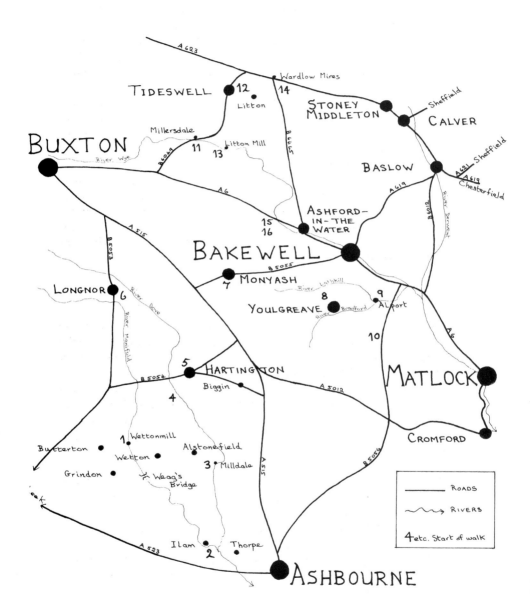

INTRODUCTION

Though the walks in this guide are by no means exclusive to families they were mapped out with the whims, interests and stamina of children at heart. The more strenuous sections tend, on the whole, to come within the first half of a walk, with easier, often downhill walking to finish. Pubs and teashops en route are in most cases about half to two-thirds of the way along. Road walking has been kept to a minimum, and most routes avoid this altogether. In addition to stops for refreshment all the walks have several focal points attractive to children, such as caves, rivers and streams, weirs and fishpools, rocks for scrambling, fossils, old mine workings, and so on.

The White Peak covers a third of the Peak District National Park and takes its name from the limestone rocks of this central area. In contrast to the bleaker moorland scenery of the surrounding mass of the Dark Peak, it offers a somewhat gentler landscape. A plateau cut by narrow, winding, and wooded river valleys, with numerous small, ancient settlements, it has the necessary ingredients for some of the most scenically varied and interesting walking in the country.

Choosing a walk

Unless the children taking part are seasoned walkers, try not to be too ambitious. Most children are used to walking to the shops or a nearby park, but continuous walking along uneven and sometimes muddy footpaths is quite a different matter.

With the very young, the three to six year olds, start by walking interesting parts of routes, and always be prepared to turn back. Make contingency plans so that if the party gets half way, and the little ones are on the point of rebellion, rescue can be arranged by meeting motorised friends at the pub en route, or by one of the party making haste back to collect the transport.

Whilst some five year olds well-accustomed to country walks can manage a four mile trek up hill and down dale, a seven or eight year old doing it for the first time may well find the same walk close to his or her limit. I would advise that newcomers start with the shorter, easier walks, and build up gradually to the more strenuous ones. A mile and a half can make all the difference to a small pair of legs! At the back of the book you will find a list of the routes in order of difficulty. This, of course, is a purely personal assessment, and other opinions may vary slightly from my own.

Allowing sufficient time

Each walk is intended as the best part of a day's outing, allowing time for play, exploration and rest stops. It is better to over-estimate rather than underestimate the time it may take, and then have to 'route-march' the latter part of the journey. As every parent knows there are good days and bad days, good moods and bad moods, and the pace will be dictated by such factors. A small child with only its boring parents for company may decide to play up and demand to be carried, whilst the same child in the company of other children may be spurred on to do great deeds. Taking all in all, I would reckon on a pace of around one mile per hour for the very young, graduating to two miles per hour for the seasoned eleven year old.

What to wear

British weather being what it is, it is best to go prepared for the worst, and even on a dry day there is always the chance that a youngster will end up soaked if the walk follows a river or stream. For the grown-ups traditional hiking boots are best, though any comfortable, waterproof shoes with a good grip will do. Children quickly grow out of expensive walking boots, so trainer-type shoes with wellington boots as back-up are adequate. Waterproof outer clothes are essential for every member of the party - never rely on it not to rain! A spare sweater for the youngsters is advisable, and a complete change of clothing is a must for the more accident-prone little ones. If the walks are being attempted in the colder months, make sure that the children are very well wrapped up to begin with - a child loses heat more rapidly than the average healthy adult.

The weather

In the Peak District, both during and after prolonged wet spells, footpaths can become extremely muddy and slippery, and stepping stones can be covered by several inches of water. This should be considered when choosing a route. On the other hand, if you wait for the skies to clear many opportunities will be missed. Gloomy weather out in the country is not half as bad as in the city. Just make sure the party is well insulated, and be prepared to lower your sights for the day.

Public rights of way

All the walks in this guide follow public rights of way or concessionary footpaths. However, on parts of several routes, due to infrequent use, there is little trace of the path. In some cases the right of way may lead straight across a cultivated field. So long as you walk in the direction described in this guide, you will be keeping to the right of way.

Should you take any other line — around the field perimeter, for instance — you would be trespassing. If a farmer has blocked off a stile on a public right of way with no indication of another way through, use your initiative but avoid damage to walls and fences.

The maps

The maps in this guide in combination with the route descriptions are sufficiently detailed to be used without reference to any other maps of the area.

Refreshments

Most of the pubs en route allow children accompanied by adults into their premises. Many also have beer-gardens, whilst at others a village green serves the same purpose. In the few cases where children are not allowed inside, the pubs are mentioned nevertheless, since their locations are sufficently pleasant to drink and relax outside if the weather is good.

If a packed lunch is carried remember that most licensees do not approve of own food being consumed on the premises. If you intend buying pub food remember that catering often ceases half an hour or so before closing time.

Teashop opening times vary according to the time of year and expected volume of custom, but most can be relied upon to be open until five or six o'clock during the summer season.

Transport to the area

Although I have assumed that most people will travel to the area by car, a fair number of the starts of walks can be reached by bus. In some others it is possible to start and finish at another point along the walk, where there is a bus stop. Brief details are given at the end of the route descriptions, and there is a list of bus operators at the back of the book.

LAPWING   Black and white 30cm.

7

Symbols used on the route maps

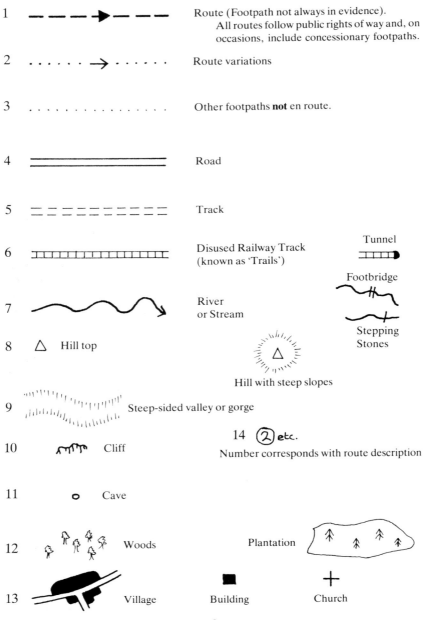

1. ▬ ▬ ▬ ▶ ▬ ▬ ▬   Route (Footpath not always in evidence). All routes follow public rights of way and, on occasions, include concessionary footpaths.

2. · · · · · · → · · · · · ·   Route variations

3. · · · · · · · · · · · · · · · · · · ·   Other footpaths **not** en route.

4. ═══════════   Road

5. ═ ═ ═ ═ ═ ═ ═ ═ ═ ═   Track

6. ⊞⊞⊞⊞⊞⊞⊞⊞⊞⊞   Disused Railway Track (known as 'Trails')

    Tunnel
    ⊞⊞⊞▶

7. River or Stream

    Footbridge

    Stepping Stones

8. △ Hill top

    △ Hill with steep slopes

9. Steep-sided valley or gorge

10. ⋀⋀⋀ Cliff

14. ② etc.
Number corresponds with route description

11. ● Cave

12. Woods

    Plantation

13. Village

    ■ Building

    ✝ Church

8

Thor's Cave and Ossom's Hill

Outline   Wettonmill ~ Thor's Cave ~ Grindon ~ Wettonmill.

Summary   The first part of the walk follows the course of the former Leek and Manifold Valley Light Railway through an impressive valley with steep wooded slopes, and dominated by the huge cliff with the gaping entrance to Thor's cave. After this, the nature of the walk changes as it follows less well-trodden footpaths through woods and meadows into the tiny village of Grindon. The way back is along a track at first, then through fields with stiles along the upper flanks of Ossom's Hill, with breathtaking views of the surrounding hills and valleys. A steep grassy descent then leads straight down to Wettonmill.

Attractions   Wettonmill, whose name derives from a 19th century cornmill, now a farm and tea shop, is a popular riverside picnic spot. The cave behind the tea shop, used as a rock shelter by Stone Age hunter-gatherers, is safe and interesting to investigate. It is also worthwhile to scramble up to a vantage point above the cave, for the view down the valley to Thor's Cave. Those who are nervous of heights should avoid this excursion, and youngsters should be accompanied. Take special care in or after wet weather - limestone becomes extremely slippery.

The walk down the Manifold Valley is along a former railway track, now an asphalt footpath. Closed in 1934, the light railway used to transport milk from farms bordering on the valley to the main line station at Waterhouses, from where it would continue its journey for distribution in the towns of North Staffordshire. On summer weekends and in the holiday season it was also used to transport tourists to Thor's Cave, a gaping hole set high in a limestone cliff that rises 300 feet from the valley bottom. The view from the cave entrance is one of the finest in the Peak District, making the stiff climb up to it well worth the effort. Judging by its proportions - it is over 30 feet in height - the cave must have been part of a system that once carried a considerable flow of water. Though often muddy, it is interesting to explore, especially with the knowledge that it was used, along with the adjacent Thor's Fissure and Elderbush Caves as a shelter by Stone Age hunters on the trail of bison and reindeer. Relics found here indicate that the caves were also used during Roman and Anglo-Saxon times, though for what purpose is not known. A collection of some of the finds excavated here are on display in Buxton Museum.

continued on page 12

9

Route 1

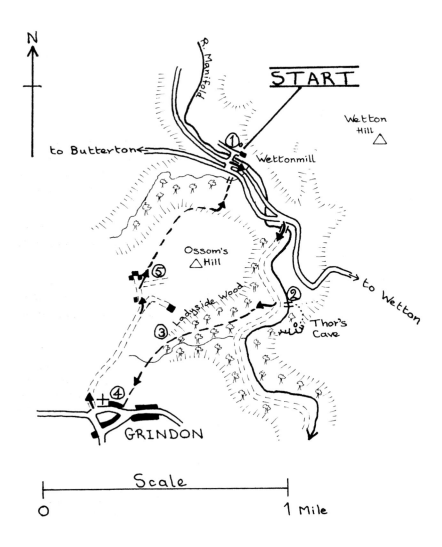

Route 1

Thor's Cave and Ossom's Hill   3¼ miles

START   *At Wettonmill in the Manifold Valley.* (G.R. 095561)

ROUTE

1. *From the riverside car park, follow either of two roads south (i.e. downstream) to where they meet. Leave the road at this point and cross the river by the little bridge. Continue along the metalled footpath to a footbridge on the left in ½ mile. Cross this and follow the obvious footpath up to Thor's Cave. Retrace your steps to the metalled footpath.*

2. *Instead of turning left to continue down the valley, cross the stile immediately facing, which gives access to a footpath leading up the valley side opposite Thor's Cave. Follow this path up the hill steeply at first, then into Ladyside Wood. On emerging from the wood at a stile, the footpath becomes less distinct.*

3. *Bear slightly right, then walk directly towards a row of cottages in the distance, keeping right of a gully. Leave the field by a stile immediately left of the cottages.*

4. *Go left at the road, then keep right to reach the Cavalier Inn. Continue towards the church, taking the lane which bypasses it on the left. Follow this for ½ mile, then take the track which forks left, passing a prominent barn.*

5. *Immediately before the farm ahead is a track leading uphill to the right. Ignore this. Instead, bear right to an obvious stile just to the right of the farm. Cross it and continue in the same general direction through fields with stiles, keeping just below the summit of Ossom's Hill. On reaching a fence, follow it down steep ground to a stile, then continue along the other side of the fence to a footbridge and the start.*

CURLEW   Speckled brown 55cm.

11

After the early climax of the visit to Thor's Cave, the scramble up the hillside opposite through Ladyside Wood, followed by refreshments in the beer garden at the Cavalier Inn at Grindon, should be sufficient to sustain enthusiasm. Incidentally, the inn was inappropriately named, presumably by latter-day Royalists, since this area was a Roundhead stronghold.

For the young birdwatcher, there is plenty to see en route. But since many of the species are small woodland birds, it is best to carry field glasses and a pocket guide. One of the commonest varieties is the grey wagtail as it flits about beside the river. The river itself may or may not be in evidence depending on the weather, for in prolonged dry spells it disappears underground to reappear near Ilam a few miles downstream. More often heard than seen, the green woodpecker inhabits the woods in the locality and, on the return along Ossom's Hill, keep an eye out for curlew and wheatear.

On a fine summer's day, the river at Wettonmill is an ideal place for children to splash around, and makes for a suitable ending to an enjoyable little walk.

Refreshments Cavalier Inn, Grindon. Children admitted, beer garden, tea, coffee, snacks and meals available.

Tea-shop, Wettonmill.

LION'S HEAD, DOVEDALE

12

Route 2

Dove Dale and Ilam Tops

Outline   Dove Dale Car Park ~ Ilam Rock ~ Ilam Tops ~ Car Park

(not recommended for children under 9)

Summary   The route follows a well used and often muddy footpath along a gorge for two miles, passing some of the most interesting rock scenery in the limestone dales. At a footbridge below Ilam Rock, a prominent pinnacle, the river is crossed, whence a very steep scramble through Dovedale Wood leads in 400 feet to a footpath clinging to the top of the wood and the rim of the gorge. Before breaking away over a ridge to the high pastures of Ilam Tops, one is rewarded for the effort of reaching this point by a quite exceptional view of the dale below. From Ilam Tops, the route follows footpaths down through meadows before skirting the steep-sided Bunster Hill and returning across more fields to the start.

Attractions   The gorge has some spectacular rock scenery. Limestone spires and other weird, natural rock sculptures tower above the river, and the heavily wooded slopes camouflage their presence until one is almost upon them. The main features are marked on the accompanying map, the names of which clearly describe their peculiar attributes. The tors and spires are regularly visited by rock climbers on dry, summer weekends and provide entertainment for onlookers. The nose and chin of Lion's Head Rock, not marked on the map, is clearly discernible, the footpath passing directly below it. Ilam Rock is quite a spectacular monolith detached from the valley side. Several rock climbs of varying degrees of difficulty lead to its summit, from which escape is by abseil.

The limestone in the dale is riddled with caves and potholes. Probably the most interesting diversion for energetic youngsters is to Reynard's Cave, which has a natural arch as a gateway. Arrow heads, pottery and other relics dating back to the early Roman occupation have been excavated from the cave, and these are on display at Buxton Museum. A word of caution; in or immediately after wet weather, take special care hereabouts, since limestone becomes extremely slippery in these conditions.

The scramble up behind Ilam Rock is initially quite steep and hard-going, tree roots aiding progress - an exciting way out of the gorge. However, special care must be taken not to dislodge stones and other

continued on page 16

13

Route 2

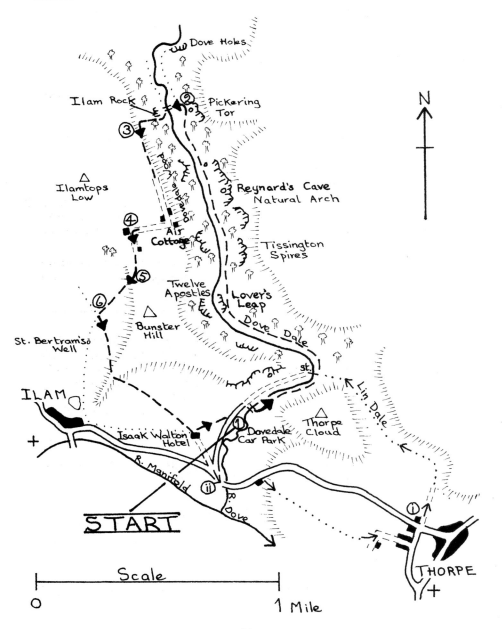

N

Dove Holes

Ilam Rock

Pickering Tor

②

③

Ilamtops Low

Reynard's Cave
Natural Arch

④

Air Cottage

Tissington Spires

⑤

Twelve Apostles

Lover's Leap

⑥

Bunster Hill

Dove Dale

St. Bertram's Well

st.

Lin Dale

ILAM

Isaak Walton Hotel

Thorpe Cloud

①

Dovedale Car Park

R. Manifold

ⓘⓘ

R. Dove

START

THORPE

Scale

0   1 Mile

14

Route 2
Dove Dale and Ilam Tops

4½ miles

(Longer variation 6 miles)

START   *At Dove Dale car park near the Izaak Walton Hotel, situated halfway between Ilam and Thorpe (G.R. 147508)*

ROUTE

1. *From the car park, follow the metalled track upstream to a footbridge. Either cross the river here or at stepping stones a little further on, then follow the footpath along Dove Dale for two miles to a footbridge at the foot of Ilam Rock, a prominent limestone pinnacle on the opposite bank.*

2. *Cross the river and scramble up the very steep wooded slope just to the left of the pinnacle.*

3. *At the top go left along a footpath which clings to the top of Dove Dale wood. In ¼ mile, the path joins a track. Follow this through a farm, passing Air Cottage on the left, and continue, now at right angles to the dale, towards another farm at Ilam Tops.*

4. *Immediately before the farm, turn left along a track running parallel to an avenue of trees. Go through a gate, passing a barn on the left, and continue in the same direction to a stile.*

5. *Cross this and bear right, following the wall down to a footpath which crosses at right angles.*

6. *Turn left here and follow the path across the steep flanks of Bunster Hill to reach a gap in the ridge ahead. Descend to a wall and a stile. Cross this, ignoring the well-trodden footpath following the line of the wall, and head straight for the farm buildings which are situated at the back of the Izaak Walton Hotel. When adjacent to the hotel a footpath bears to the left to finish at the car park. (A stile gives access to the hotel for those seeking refreshment).*

VARIATION

The route can be lengthened by 1½ miles by starting and finishing at Thorpe, a much quieter place than Dove Dale Car Park.

Find a suitable place to park in the village, then:

i. *Take the footpath from the small car park by the public toilets in the village, signposted Dove Dale, and follow it to where it joins the other route at the stepping stones. Continue as above to the Izaak Walton Hotel, then on down the drive to the road.*

ii. *Turn left and either follow the road back up into Thorpe or take the road as far as the cattle grid, pass through the gate, and bear right immediately up the very steep hillside to a stile at the top. Continue in the same direction to join a track which leads back into the village.*

debris on to unsuspecting parties below. Should this happen, a loud "BELOW!" will alert potential victims to the danger.

A reward for the effort of the climb out of the gorge, more attractive to the younger specimens than a fine view of the wonders below, is the assortment of refreshments offered at the nearby Air Cottage.

The way back is in sharp contrast to what has gone before. Mainly downhill, the route traces its way through open fields, though a short section involves traversing the steep flanks of Bunster Hill. Directly below this, though hardly worth the effort of descending to it and having to climb back up the hill, is St Bertram's Well, now a cattle trough. St Bertram was an early Christian missionary to the area and his tomb can be seen in the church near Ilam Hall.

Wildlife in the gorge is plentiful and easily spotted. In particular, look out for dippers and water vole on the river. On the thickly wooded slopes are all manner of birds, some of which are mentioned in the following walk, Route 3. Equipment, luck, time of day and the weather will determine which of these are seen.

For those interested in prehistoric wildlife, the screes on the slopes of Thorpe Cloud are rich in fossil shellfish. These were deposited when the hill was a reef in a tropical sea which covered the area around 350 million years ago.

Refreshments Air Cottage, Ilam Tops, tea, coffee and scones on sale in season.

Izaak Walton Hotel. Children admitted, beer garden, tea and coffee served all day, bar snacks and lunches available.

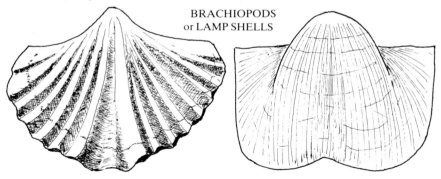

BRACHIOPODS
or LAMP SHELLS

ACCESS BY BUS

To Ilam or Thorpe, from Manchester, Buxton, Ashbourne & Derby (Trent), and from Chesterfield & Bakewell (Silver Service). In each case, summer Sundays and Bank Holidays only.

Upper Dove Dale and Hall Dale

Outline   Milldale ~ Ilam Rock ~ Stanshope ~ Alstonefield ~ Milldale

Summary   This walk complements Route 2, taking in the upper part of Dove Dale. Though not quite so spectacular, it is never without interest and is less strenuous. A footpath is followed from Milldale as far as the footbridge below Ilam Rock, passing the impressive Dove Holes en route. The river is crossed at this point and Hall Dale, a tributary of the Dove, is entered. A less well used footpath gradually ascends the dry valley to where it ends at Stanshope, a cluster of farms. From here, a track leads down to the minor road which runs through Sunny Bank, another dry valley which joins the Dove at Milldale - thereby providing an escape route if required. A short, steep footpath is then followed up the opposite side of the valley to meadows and a track into Alstonefield, one of the most attractive villages in the White Peak. It is left by an ancient packhorse trail that leads comfortably back down to Milldale, and from which there are particularly good views of the dramatic scenery at the head of Dove Dale.

Attractions   Milldale is a busy little stopping off point for tourists and has a tea shop. Its main attraction, other than its quaintness, is its position at the head of Dove Dale, entry to which is by an ancient packhorse bridge which linked the trail from Alstonefield to Tissington. The bridge is mentioned by Izaak Walton (see Route 4) in his book "The Compleat Angler" in a reference to a conversation between "Piscator et Viator", an angler and a traveller. Apparently, the traveller thought the bridge a joke, and commented on how people in these parts must travel in wheelbarrows, the bridge being so narrow. Hence the bridge came to be known as Viator Bridge.

En route through Dove Dale the footpath passes Dove Holes, two huge but shallow cavities etched out by the river thousands of years ago. Inside, there are several nooks and crannies to explore, and a 10 minute halt is statutory. On the opposite side of the river is Raven's Tor, an impressive limestone cliff occasionally visited by rock climbers. Rising like a huge monolith above the footbridge, and best viewed from the south, is Ilam Rock, a limestone pinnacle with several rock climbs to its summit.

Once into Hall Dale, people become scarce. An interesting quarter of an hour can be spent in the relative quiet rummaging for the fossil

continued on page 20

17

Route 3

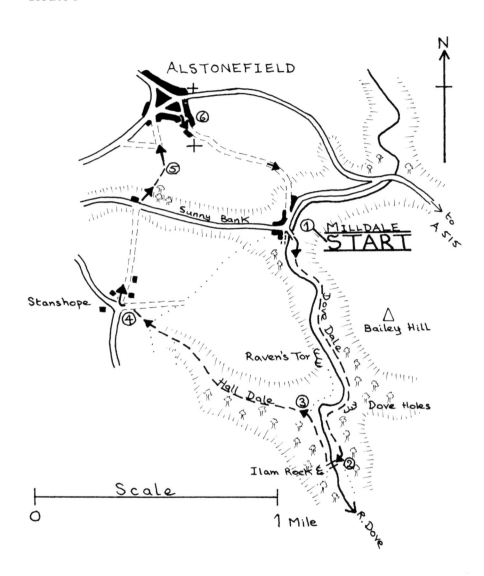

Route 3

Upper Dove Dale and Hall Dale

4½ miles

START   *At Milldale, 1½ miles off the A 515, 5 miles north of Ashbourne.* (G.R. 139547)

ROUTE

1. *Cross the packhorse bridge to enter Dove Dale and follow the riverside footpath for about 1½ miles to the footbridge at the foot of Ilam Rock, a prominent limestone pinnacle on the opposite bank.*
2. *Cross it, turn right, and walk back upstream for ¼ mile to where Hall Dale joins Dove Dale on the left.*
3. *Turn left and follow the ascending footpath through Hall Dale. Where it peters out, continue in the same direction through fields, heading for the cluster of buildings which is Stanshope.*
4. *On reaching a track, turn left, and in a few metres turn sharp right to follow another track past farms. This leads down to the minor road at Sunny Bank. Go straight across to the stile opposite and gain the footpath which ascends to the right by a wall. Follow the wall as it bends round to the left. Continue over a stile to the corner of a large field on the far side of which is the church at Alstonefield.*
5. *Turn left, and follow the wall on the left to a stile and a track. Go straight on and into Alstonefield.*
6. *To continue, take the minor road which leads to the old church,* **not** *to the more recent Methodist church. This soon degenerates into a track which is followed down into Milldale. A footpath to the right just after the church graveyard, signposted Milldale, leads more directly back to the start.*

SHORTER VARIATION

As for 1 to 4 above as far as Sunny Bank, then turn right to return to Milldale.

ACCESS BY BUS

To Alstonefield only, from Chesterfield & Bakewell (Silver Service), summer Sundays and Bank Holidays only.

remains of prehistoric shellfish deposited when the whole of this area was submerged beneath a tropical sea.

Alstonefield is a very attractive village with several interesting buildings (see Route 4). On leaving the most welcoming of these, try to fit in a visit to the old church. If you are carrying binoculars, look carefully at the date above the main porch on the large old farm on the left just before the church.

Despite the volume of human traffic through Dove Dale, the dipper is the most commonly seen waterside bird. Out of season, the heron feels more secure and seems not to be put off by the occasional traveller. A more trained eye is needed to identify some of the other species in the dale, which include redstart, bullfinch and marsh tit. Should you be very lucky and looking skyward, you may be treated with a glimpse of a bird not often seen in these parts - the buzzard.

Refreshments George Inn, Alstonefield. Children admitted, beer garden, tea, coffee, snacks available.

Tea shops at Alstonefield and Milldale.

ALSTONEFIELD CHURCH

Route 4

(Variation 5 miles)

Wolfscote Dale and Narrow Dale

Outline   Beaver Ford ~ Coldeaton Bridge ~ Alstonefield ~ Narrow Dale ~ Beaver Ford.

(not recommended for children under 9 unless variation is taken)

Summary   The route follows a path by the River Dove through an attractive winding gorge which, in parts narrows to the width of the river. After passing through a wooded section a footbridge is crossed, and a very steep grassy ascent of the valley side follows. When passable, however, a much less strenuous way up is to cross the river by stepping stones further upstream and take a more gradually ascending footpath. Whichever route is chosen, footpaths and tracks through meadowland lead on from here into the unspoilt village of Alstonefield. The route then follows a minor road for ¾ mile, before breaking away across more meadows towards Narrow Dale, a tiny valley flanked by a hill on each side. The last section is no more than a pleasant stroll along an old and little used farm track which leads comfortably back to the start.

Attractions   One of the narrowest of the dales, Wolfscote Dale offers ever changing scenery throughout its length. The valley sides are always steep and, in places, craggy. Near the start of the walk, and at the foot of a tall cliff to the left of the footpath, is a cave through which a small individual can pass relatively easily to emerge at another point a little further along. Larger specimens should hand over the torch at this point and await re-emergence of the offspring at the exit, which would be a tight, and possibly embarrassing, squeeze. Another cave just beyond the point at which Biggin Dale joins Wolfscote Dale is no more than a shallow depression but the view from its entrance is worth the diversion. Where the footpath crosses scree, stop to rummage through the debris for the fossil remains of shellfish that date back more than 300 million years. Also of interest to the naturalist are the rare as well as common alpines which find the sheltered slopes an ideal habitat. Left undisturbed, they will flourish for years to come.

Footbridges, stepping stones, weirs and the trout pools created by them make the river an attractive proposition for children. The keen angler might be interested to know that this was a favourite haunt of Izaak Walton, 17th century angler and author of "The Compleat Angler". At

continued on page 24

21

Route 4

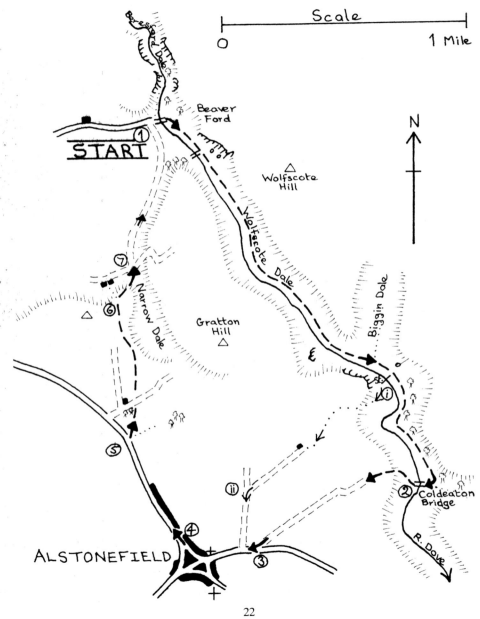

Scale

O   1 Mile

N

Beaver Ford

START ①

Wolfscote Hill

Wolfscote Dale

Biggin Dale

Narrow Dale

Gratton Hill

⑦

⑥

(i)

(ii)

⑤

② Coldeaton Bridge

R. Dove

④

ALSTONEFIELD

③

Route 4

Wolfscote Dale and Narrow Dale

5½ miles

(Variation 5 miles)

START   *To get to Beaver Ford (not marked on either the One Inch Tourist Map of the Peak District or the 1:25000 Outdoor Leisure Map of the White Peak) turn left off the B 5054 1¼ miles west of Hartington in the direction of Hulme End. The narrow lane is signposted Beresford Dale. Follow it, keeping left, to its end. The walk starts here.* (G.R. 128586)

ROUTE

1. *Cross the footbridge and go right. In a short distance is another footbridge. Disregard this and continue along the well-trodden footpath, passing Biggin Dale on the left, to a third footbridge.*

2. *Cross it and go straight up the very steep grass slope, keeping just right of a shallow gully which may or may not have a stream. Continue over a stile, along a walled footpath, then a track, to a minor road.*

3. *Turn right into the village. The George Inn is on the left.*

4. *Keep right and follow the road, signposted Hulme End, for about ¼ mile beyond the last buildings to a prominent left-hand bend and a stile on the right.*

5. *Turn right and cross a field, heading for the corner of a small wood. Cross a track and continue in the same direction along a well-stiled footpath to a stile in a wall on the right.*

6. *Turn right and descend into the tiny dale (Narrow Dale). Follow it down to a track.*

7. *Keep straight on. The track leads back to the start.*

VARIATION

This is a less strenuous way out of Wolfscote Dale.

As for 1 above to the stepping stones 200 metres beyond the entrance to Biggin Dale, then:

i. *Cross the river by the stepping stones and follow the footpath up to the left to a stile at the top. Continue bearing left towards a prominent barn. Follow a track from here to where this joins another track.*

ii. *Turn left, and follow it to a road, then as for 3 to 7 above.*

points along the river bank, nature has provided natural lawns perfect for a picnic and an excuse to watch for waterfowl and dipper.

Alstonefield is a delightful little village with its old stone cottages and farm buildings. Of especial interest are an Elizabethan Manor House, dated 1587, now a farm house, and the old church, which is late 16th century and a real gem. A three-storey building a little way on from the Post Office used to be a workhouse where the inmates polished locally quarried limestone for decorative use.

Refreshments George Inn, Alstonefield. Children admitted, beer garden, tea, coffee and snacks available.

Tea shop at Alstonefield.

HARTINGTON

24

Beresford Dale and Biggin Dale

Outline
Hartington ~ Beresford Dale ~ Wolfscote Dale ~ Biggin Dale ~ Hartington.

Summary   Sharing Wolfscote Dale with the previous route, this walk takes in two other quite contrasting limestone valleys, Beresford Dale and Biggin Dale, and remains on the Derbyshire side of the River Dove. Beresford Dale is short but a true gorge with steep, wooded slopes, cliffs and a winding stretch of river, whilst Biggin Dale is more open and less oppressive, with scant vegetation covering scree slopes, and is usually dry for most of its length. The stretch from Dale End to Hartington follows an old track from which there are panoramic views of the limestone plateau and the prominent hills around. The footpath through Wolfscote Dale can be muddy and slippery during and after wet weather.

Attractions   Beresford Dale is a fairy-tale gorge, winding and wooded with jutting, limestone buttresses, a rock spire that seems to be growing out of the river — the 'Pike' in 'Pike Pool' — and a mysterious looking building half-hidden by trees. The little building is, in fact, Charles Cotton's Fishing House, erected in 1674, and designed as a cosy base for his, and his friend Isaak Walton's fishing exploits in the dale. Cotton inherited Beresford Hall, which no longer stands, but was forced to sell the estate to settle his debts. However, for many years he succeeded in avoiding his creditors by hiding out in a cave on the estate.

If time is available, it is well worth stopping to catch a glimpse of the birdlife in this wooded dale. Dippers are common and a treat to watch as they disappear into the river to re-emerge a little further on. The grey wagtail, its grey upper parts distinguishing it from the yellow wagtail, is a summer visitor. Less easily spotted are the tree-creeper as well as various types of warbler.

Wolfscote Dale is essentially the continuation of Beresford Dale, and along this stretch the river has formed a narrow, winding valley, much of which is treeless. The yew, however, unlike in most of the other limestone dales, has not been usurped by the ash, and can be seen growing from some of the cliff faces. Specific points of interest are described for the previous walk.

continued on page 28

25

Route 5

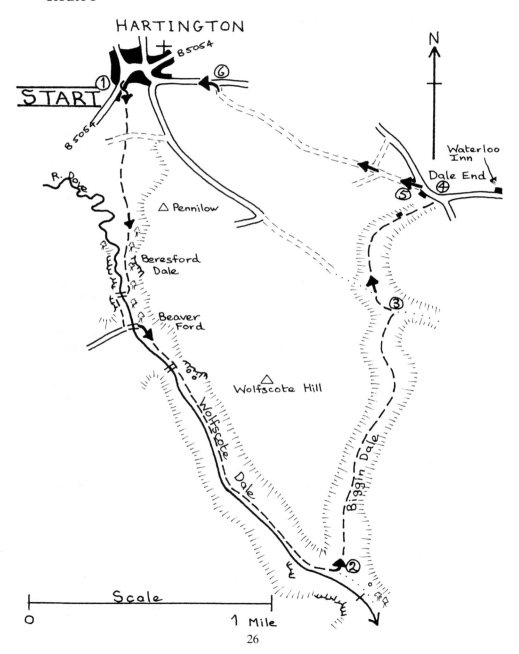

HARTINGTON

B5054

START ①

B5054

⑥

N

Waterloo Inn

Dale End

⑤

④

R. Dove

△ Pennilow

Beresford Dale

Beaver Ford

Wolfscote Hill △

Wolfscote Dale

Biggin Dale

③

②

Scale

0   1 Mile

Route 5

Beresford Dale and Biggin Dale

6 miles

START   *At Hartington* (G.R. 127604)

ROUTE

1. *50 metres past the Charles Cotton Hotel in the direction of Hulme End, and on the opposite side of the road, a footpath, signposted Beresford Dale, leads off left by the public toilets. Turn right behind the building. Follow the path across fields, cross a track, and continue into the gorge of Beresford Dale.*

   Follow the obvious footpath through the dale, first on the left bank, then on the right, to a second footbridge. This is at Beaver Ford. Cross it and continue once more on the left bank to where Biggin Dale joins Wolfscote Dale on the left.

2. *Go left and follow the dale to where it branches.*

3. *Take the left branch, signposted Hartington, and follow it to its end, ignoring a footpath going left a little way further on, and also signposted Hartington.*

4. *On reaching the end of Biggin (Dale End), turn right at the road, then left into Biggin Dale to the Waterloo Inn. Retrace your steps to Dale End.*

5. *Take the first track left by the old cottage. Ignore a left fork at the brow of the hill, and keep straight on. Follow this track to its end, where it joins a minor road.*

6. *Turn left and continue down the hill into Hartington.*

SHORTER VARIATION

As for 1 to 3 above as far as the second signposted path which you are instructed to ignore in the longer walk. Take this path. Continue to and along a track, then a lane back into Hartington.

ACCESS BY BUS

To Hartington from Buxton & Ashbourne (Warrington), Saturdays only. Also from Chesterfield & Bakewell (Silver Service), and from Manchester, Buxton, Ashbourne & Derby (Trent), in each case summer Sundays and Bank Holidays only.

Biggin Dale is a gentler version of Wolfscote Dale without the stream. Its upper reaches provide sheltered, safe areas ideal for a picnic. There is a cave en route, probably mined in the past, and the screes are rich in fossils. The upper part of the dale is a nature reserve and is the habitat of several species of wildflower. Look out for wrens on the walls by the footpath and hares on the upper slopes.

Refreshments Waterloo Inn at Biggin. Children admitted, beer garden, snacks available, open all day for tea and coffee.

Charles Cotton Hotel at Hartington. Children admitted, beer garden, lunches and snacks available.

Devonshire Arms at Hartington. Children's room with assortment of games, outdoor seating, bar snacks available.

Tea shops at Hartington.

COBBLED
STREET IN
LONGNOR

Route 6

Longnor and Earl Sterndale

Outline   Longnor ~ Parkhouse Hill ~ Earl Sterndale ~ Longnor

Summary   An interesting route in some of the most attractive countryside in the White Peak. Cut off from the main tourist centres it also remains one of the quieter areas for walking and exploring. The route follows footpaths and tracks all but for ¼ mile of road. From Longnor, a descent is made to the wide and fertile farmland in the upper reaches of the valley formed by the River Dove. The river is crossed near the impressive jagged peaks of Chrome Hill and Parkhouse Hill, the view from the latter being one of the best in the Peak Park. However, the owner of the hill seems less than keen to share this privilege with the walking public and has erected large signs to this effect. From this beautiful spot, a short ascent up the flanks of Hitter Hill leads into Earl Sterndale. On from here, the route descends into the valley again and the quiet pastures by the River Dove. Another footbridge leads back over the river, and the route continues up the opposite side of the valley into Longnor. After wet weather some of the lower level parts of the walk can be extremely muddy or wet underfoot.

Attractions   After crossing the River Dove at the first footbridge a scout should be sent ahead to reconnoitre the driest route through the boggy ground bordering the river. Once this problem has been overcome and the metalled track reached, the party can pause to take in the splendid surroundings. Straight ahead is the jagged ridge of Parkhouse Hill. To the left is Chrome Hill and between them lies the secluded Dowel Dale. There are only a handful of peaks in the Peak District, and these occur mainly in the limestone White Peak. In the Lakeland fells and Snowdonia, volcanic outpourings followed by uplift of the land and erosion by ice and water produced the mountain peaks. Such phenomena as Chrome Hill and Parkhouse Hill, however, grew as reefs about 350 million years ago when this part of the world was submerged beneath a tropical sea.

Less than ½ mile on from Parkhouse Hill, in Dowel Dale, is Dowel Cave, which can be explored by torchlight for a few metres. It was used by nomads of the Old as well as the New Stone Age as a rock shelter during hunting forays in the area, and the skeletons of ten individuals were unearthed during excavation. Alongside the bodies, flints, a bone pin and food offerings were found. No doubt the hunters who used the cave

continued on page 32

Route 6

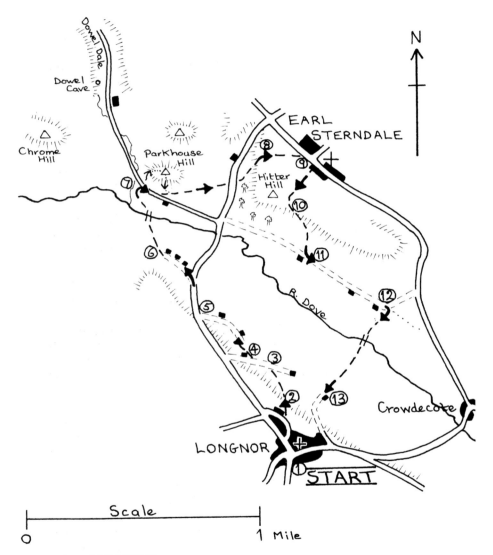

ACCESS BY BUS
  To Longnor from Derby & Ashbourne (Trent), summer Sundays and
  Bank Holidays only.

Route 6
Longnor and Earl Sterndale

4½ miles

START *At Longnor.* (G.R. 088649)

ROUTE

1. *From the square, walk up Buxton Rd. to Church St. on the right. Take the narrow lane that joins Church St. near its junction with the main road and follow it to where it bends left in front of bungalows. Take the footpath up to the right to a stile on the left, and continue alongside the bungalows. Keep straight on through a field to a stile.*

2. *Bear left downhill to reach a track.*

3. *Turn left and follow the track to a recently renovated farm building in 200 metres.*

4. *Leave the track at this point and pass just to the right of the building. Continue in this direction to a wooden stile in the hedge on the right. Cross it and continue past a house, then follow a track for ¼ mile up to the main road.*

5. *Turn right along the road, then take the first track to the left. Where the track bends right, go straight on over a stile. Continue in the same direction, passing through a keyhole stile and crossing an old hedgerow.*

6. *After the hedgerow, bear right downhill towards a footbridge. Cross it and continue in the same direction to a white painted stile and a track. (Parkhouse Hill is directly ahead).*

7. *Turn right and bear left off the track to a gateway and stile. Continue in the same direction to another stile. Cross the main road to the stile opposite, then bear left up the hill (Hitter Hill). Where it steepens, continue ascending the hill more or less directly to reach a white stile at the top.*

8. *Bear right and continue through fields to Earl Sterndale.*

9. *Turn right at the road, and go as far as the Quiet Woman. Walk around the pub to the right, and follow the footpath, signposted Crowdecote, through fields to a second signpost, where the footpath trends left to a stile with a handrail.*

10. *Follow the wall on the left for 40 metres, then bear right downhill to a stile at the bottom. Continue to a track by a cottage.*

11. *Turn left and follow this for ½ mile to where it bends sharp left.*

12. *Turn right, signposted Longnor, and continue down a narrow field to a footbridge over the River Dove. Continue in the same direction uphill to a barn.*

13. *Turn left and follow the track up into Longnor to finish.*

would have had look-outs on both Parkhouse and Chrome Hills, since game could be easily spotted way down the valley.

For tired legs and parched throats a short ascent up the flanks of Hitter Hill is rewarded by refreshments at the Quiet Woman in Earl Sterndale. The headless figure on the pub sign speaks for itself.

If time permits, and home comforts can wait just a little longer, it is worth spending some time exploring the narrow cobbled streets in Longnor, a refreshing and rare phenomenon in this part of the country.

Refreshments   The Quiet Woman at Earl Sterndale.
Cheshire Cheese at Longnor.
Crewe & Harpur Arms, children admitted, tea, coffee and bar lunches available.
Cafe at Longnor.

UPPER LATHKILL DALE

32

Lathkill Dale—Upper Section

Outline   Monyash ~ Lathkill Dale ~ One Ash Grange ~ Monyash

Summary   Apart from the short section of road between the village and the start of the dale, the route follows well-trodden footpaths for the whole of its length. The first part takes one through a gradually deepening gorge with cliffs and caves, from which an escape is made up a small wooded dale on the right (Cales Dale). After passing through an ancient farm once adminstered by monks, the walk becomes a gentle stroll across meadows back to Monyash.

Attractions   This part of the dale is narrow and craggy, with plenty to keep the young explorer and naturalist occupied. The limestone screes and boulders are rich in fossils, and on the grassy slopes there are several interesting species of wild flower. Indeed for the wild flower enthusiasts, both Lathkill Dale and Cales Dale are of particular interest. As well as the more commonly seen plants, which include field scabious, meadow cranesbill, biting stone crop and hare-bell, a keen eye may spot one or two rarer species, notably Jacob's Ladder.

Lathkill Head Cave, from which springs the River Lathkill, is safe to explore near its entrance. But two other caves en route are best left for more professional exploration.

One Ash Grange is a fascinating cluster of old farm buildings with one or two other peculiar constructions. In fact, it once belonged to Roche Abbey, in Yorkshire, when it served as a penitentiary for disobedient monks. "Grange" was the term used for a house from which monks administered their land holdings. There are several in this area.

Monyash is itself, an interesting place to look around. On the green is a market cross, which dates back to the 14th century, when the village used to hold a weekly market. The church is early 13th century, and inside is a ten-foot long chest almost as old as the building itself. During the 18th and 19th centuries the village was one of the main lead-mining centres of Derbyshire.

Refreshments   The Hobbit Inn at Monyash. Children not admitted, beer garden, also village green for outside drinking, tea, coffee and bar snacks available.

Route 7

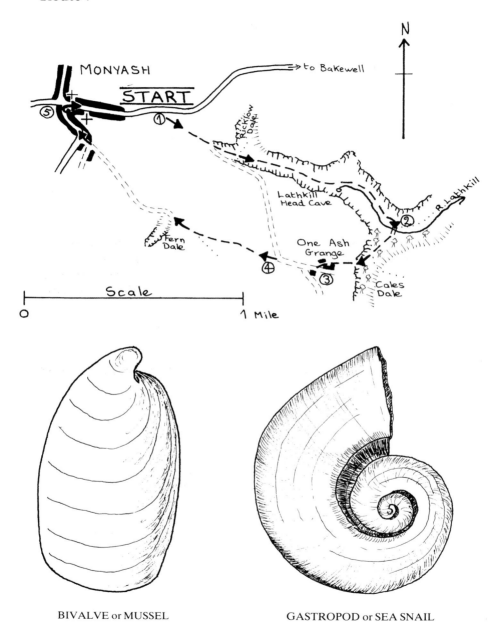

BIVALVE or MUSSEL

GASTROPOD or SEA SNAIL

34

Route 7
Lathkill Dale — Upper Section

4 miles

START   *At the head of the dale, about ½ mile from the crossroads in Monyash in the direction of Bakewell.* (G.R. 157665)

ROUTE

1. *Follow the dry valley into the gorge and continue, passing Lathkill Head Cave on the right, to a footbridge in 1½ miles.*

2. *Cross it and follow the footpath into Cales Dale. Keep right, ignoring a left fork, and continue up into One Ash Grange.*

3. *Walk through the farm, then turn right at the track. Follow it to where it bends sharp right. (To continue along the track would lead directly back to the start).*

4. *Leave the track and continue in the same direction alongside a wall on your left. After two fields the path continues along the other side of the wall and is shortly joined by another rather vague path coming from the left. After dipping down into Fern Dale the footpath joins a track. Follow this into Monyash.*

5. *Turn right at the crossroads and return to the start.*

ACCESS BY BUS

To Monyash from Chesterfield & Bakewell (Silver Service), summer Sundays and Bank Holidays only.

STONECROP
Yellow May-July

BLOODY CRANESBILL
Purple June-August

35

RUINS OF MANDALE MINE ENGINE HOUSE

Lathkill Dale — Middle Section

Outline   Moor Lane (Picnic Area) ~ Cales Dale ~ Lathkill Dale ~ Meadow Place Grange ~ Moor Lane.

Summary   An interesting walk, starting and finishing on the moor to the south of the valley, and taking in the most densely wooded part of Lathkill Dale. The river in this section is noted for its purity. The footpath through the dale is obvious and the direction into and out of the valley way-marked through fields with stiles. The walk through the dale takes in a concessionary footpath, where there is warning of the hazards of past mine workings lying close to the path. Though tempting to explore, the warning should not be taken lightly. Although most of the shafts are well capped, it is advisable to stay well away.

Attractions   The walk passes through two former monastic farms or "granges", Calling Low on the way into the valley and Meadow Place Grange on the way out. Calling Low, as with One Ash Grange, belonged to Roche Abbey in Yorkshire, whilst Meadow Place Grange was the property of Leicester Abbey. They were devoted mainly to sheep farming and were operative as such between the 12th and 16th centuries.

The dale, with a Nature Reserve on the right bank (access by special permit) has much to offer the naturalist and has an almost magical aura, with its clear stream, an enchanting weir and overgrown ruins. Only the ruins remind us of its past importance as a centre of lead-mining in the area. In the ash and elm woodland of the Nature Reserve, the scented pink mezereon, a rare British wild flower, may be found, along with many other species which also thrive alongside the footpath.

Once into the wooded section, on the concessionary footpath, shafts capped with concrete are plainly visible. This was the location of Lathkilldale lead mine. Nearby, the site of the old waterwheel pit can be seen. This housed a wheel 52 feet in diameter, once one of the largest in the country. Further downstream are the remaining pillars of an aqueduct which brought the leat to the north side of the river and Mandale lead mine, opened in 1847. Here, part of the engine house still stands. A beam engine was installed to be used when the water supply was insufficient to turn the wheel. Behind the engine house is the pumping shaft.

If the party can face the steep road up into Over Haddon, it is well worth the diversion. Aside from having the welcome oases, (a cafe and a pub) there is an especially good view of the dale and surrounding

continued on page 40

37

Route 8

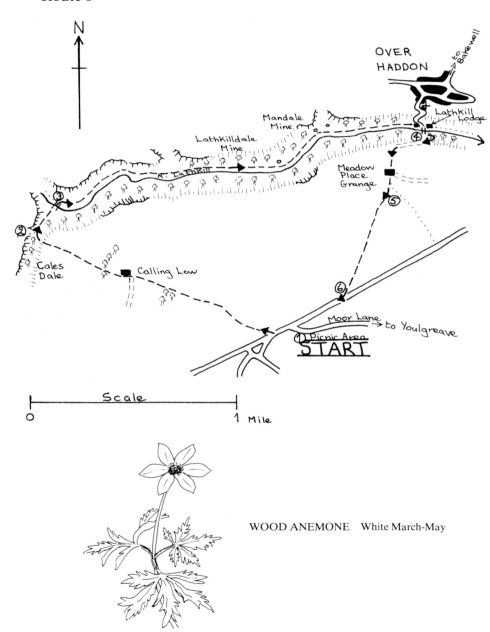

N

OVER HADDON

to Bakewell

Lathkill Lodge

Mandale Mine

Lathkilldale Mine

Lathkill

Meadow Place Grange

④⑤

⑤

③

②

Cales Dale

Calling Low

⑥

Moor Lane → to Youlgreave

Picnic Area
START

Scale

0   1 Mile

WOOD ANEMONE   White March-May

38

Route 8

Lathkill Dale — Middle Section

5½ miles

START   *1 mile west of Youlgreave at the Moor Lane Picnic Area.*
(G.R. 194645)

ROUTE

1. *From the Picnic Area walk west along Moor Lane to the T-junction in 100 metres. Immediately opposite is a stile. Cross it and head diagonally across a small field, through a gap in the wall, and continue in the same direction, using a line of stakes as guide. Carry on through the farm at Calling Low (muddy), still following the stakes, and down into Cales Dale.*

2. *After a stile turn right and continue down the tiny dale to a footbridge over the River Lathkill.*

3. *Turn right after the footbridge and follow the riverside footpath downstream for two miles to the ford and footbridge by Lathkill Lodge. (The diversion to Over Haddon is via the steep road to the left. Take the first road to the right for the pub. Retrace your steps to Lathkill Lodge.)*

4. *Cross the footbridge and follow the zigzag track to a gate and a field at the top, then bear left to the farm. Cross the courtyard and go through the gateway opposite (usually muddy).*

5. *Ignore the footpath heading straight up the hill. Instead, follow the wall on the right as it bends right (signposted Middleton) and follow more stakes across meadows with stiles to a road.*

6. *Turn right and continue along the road back to the start.*

ROCK-ROSE   Yellow May-September

countryside from this high vantage point. The village itself, a settlement since pre-Norman times, has some beautifully preserved little cottages and farm buildings. Not so old, but a fitting addition to the village, is the tiny church by the cafe.

An interesting phenomenon is experienced on the way back, both approaching and leaving Meadow Place Grange. Looking back across to Over Haddon the illusion is of fields stretching in a continuous slope up towards the village, the dale having been swallowed up.

Refreshments Lathkill Hotel at Over Haddon. Children admitted, field in front of pub, stone slab seating for outside drinkers, coffee, bar meals available.

LATHKILL DALE

Lathkill Dale — Lower Section

Outline

Alport ~ Lathkill Lodge ~ Over Haddon ~ Haddon Fields ~ Alport

Summary   The first part of the route takes a popular riverside footpath. At Alport, the valley is wide and the river flanked by meadows. But as one progresses upstream the valley sides, now wooded, begin to close in, and below Over Haddon the dale is already beginning to take on the characteristics of a gorge. From Lathkill Lodge a short steep and winding road leads up into the village. The return journey is an easy stroll through moorland pastures along a little used footpath, this linking up with the "Portway", an ancient track leading down through Haddon Fields directly to Alport.

Attractions   Alport, meaning 'old town' or 'market centre', was probably a trading post in Roman times but its location on the 'Portway', probably one of the most important prehistoric roads in The Peak District suggests it may well have been a settlement as long ago as the Bronze Age. Nowadays, it is overshadowed by Youlgreave but that is not to say it is without interest. The row of 17th and 18th century cottages on the back street by the river is quite a gem and worth a few minutes of anybody's time. The old bridge nearby complements the scene.

En route to Over Haddon the footpath passes in front of an interesting old residence in an enviable position overlooking the river, and going by the name of Raper Lodge. Nearby is a narrow packhorse bridge and further upstream is another, Conksbury Bridge, which carried the trail from Bakewell to Youlgreave over the Lathkill. The dale from Conksbury Bridge to below Over Haddon, John Merrill appropriately refers to as 'the parkland section' because the river at this point has a succession of weirs and pools bordered by wide, flat grassy stretches and tree covered slopes. The river itself is crystal clear, and the marsh marigolds put the final touches to it. Trout-spotting here is a major sport with children.

The steep climb to Over Haddon from Lathkill Lodge is, thankfully, short, though the little-legged may dispute this statement. Should persuasion be necessary, refreshments are near at hand in the village.

The walk across the moor is in complete contrast to the dale below, and the lofty situation provides panoramic views of the surrounding

continued on page 44

41

Route 9

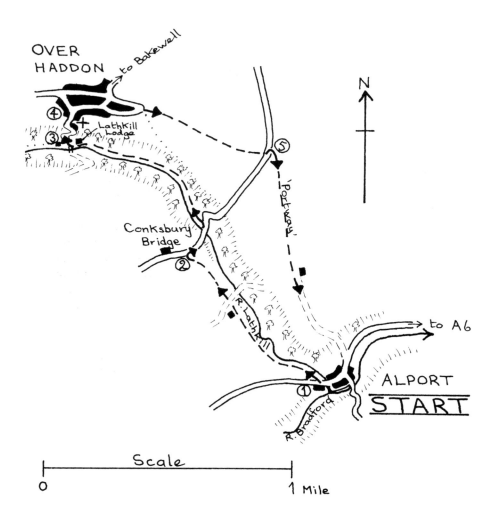

OVER HADDON

to Bakewell

④

③ ✝ Lathkill Lodge

⑤

N

Portway

Conksbury Bridge

②

R. Lathkill

to A6

ALPORT

START

①

R. Bradford

Scale

0   1 Mile

Route 9

Lathkill Dale — Lower Section

4 miles

START   *At Alport by the bridge on the main road through the village. Park at the layby. (G.R. 222645).*

ROUTE

1. *Go through the obvious stile and follow the footpath upstream on the left bank of the river. Continue across a narrow lane - this leads to a packhorse bridge on the right - to a minor road at Conksbury (1 mile).*
2. *Turn right and cross the bridge (Conksbury Bridge), then left almost immediately to follow the continuation of the footpath, now on the right bank.*
3. *At the building going by the name of Lathkill Lodge, and adjacent to which is a footbridge, turn right and continue up the steep road into Over Haddon.*
4. *Turn right at the first road on the right and keep right to reach the Lathkill Hotel. Go through the stile on the far side of the pub. Ignore the sign for Alport - this leads back down into the dale. Instead, head for the old tree straight ahead and continue in the same direction, through two open gateways, keeping close to a wall on the left, to reach a stone stile (not obvious at a distance). Bear slightly left across a field to a stile and minor road.*
5. *Turn left and follow the road for 100 metres before turning right at a gate. Continue alongside the wall on the right to farm buildings, then straight on along a track (Portway) which leads directly back down to Alport.*

ACCESS BY BUS

To Alport from Chesterfield & Bakewell, summer Sundays Bank Holidays and weekdays, and from Matlock weekdays (Silver Service).

countryside. Roman legions no longer use the 'Portway' but a parent with imagination could give a fair impression of its travellers in bygone days.

Refreshments Lathkill Hotel at Over Haddon. Children admitted, field in front of pub, stone slab seating for outside drinkers, coffee, bar meals available.

MEADOW COTTAGE, BRADFORD DALE

Route 10

Harthill Moor and Bradford Dale

Outline Robin Hood's Stride ~ Castle Ring ~ Bradford Dale ~ Hopping's Farm ~ Robin Hood's Stride

Summary The section to Youlgreave follows recognizable footpaths over Harthill Moor, and takes in several interesting features, both man-made and natural. The walk along the length of Bradford Dale provides a total contrast; a gentle limestone dale with a river whose weirs and fishpools add to its attraction. The return over the moor ascends steeply to begin with but soon levels out, and fine views across the Wye Valley make it well worth the effort. This part of the route follows a line marked by stiles, since the footpath though a public right of way, shows little evidence of being used.

Attractions The Hermit's Cave at Cratcliffe Tor, whilst hardly a cave, is worth a visit. Inside, a well preserved crucifix carved out of the rock probably dates from the 12th century, and it is interesting to ponder just how the hermitage might have looked when occupied. The Tor is popular with rock climbers and has several fine climbs of a high standard.

Best saved for the return, across from the Tor is Robin Hood's Stride, the remains of a gritstone outcrop somewhat resembling a fortress with turrets, and so named because legend has it that Robin strode from one to the other — a mere 15 metres! Though it is tempting for youngsters to climb the easier of these, a fall could prove fatal. There are ample safe boulders for the aspiring climber at a lower level.

Leaving this area, one delves into prehistory. Behind the Tor are the Nine Men, a Bronze Age stone circle. Unfortunately, only four remain standing, the other five having been conjured away. Further on is Castle Ring, the earthwork remains of an Iron Age fort.

Youlgreave is an interesting village worth exploring with cottages and farm buildings dating back to the 17th century. It also boasts a fine old church of Norman origin, though its tower is 15th century. Bradford Dale is a picturesque river valley, its slopes thickly wooded for over half its length. Below the village the river is shallow with flat, grassy banks, and is an ideal place to stop for a picnic and a paddle. Also of interest are its splendid weirs and fishpools filled with trout, an old mine, and rope swings of more recent origin -altogether a pleasant place to be on a sunny day. By the last footbridge a large detached block of limestone marks the spot where Sir Christopher Fulwood, a Royalist who had his castle at Middleton (now in ruins), was shot dead by Parliamentarians.

continued on page 48

45

Route 10

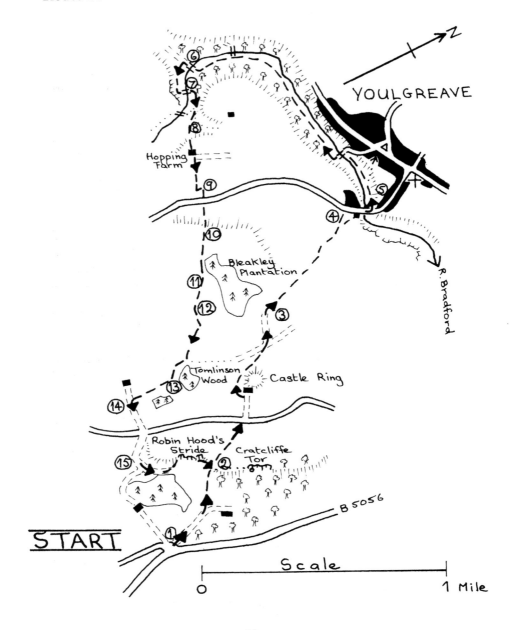

Route 10

Harthill Moor and Bradford Dale   6 miles

START   *Turn off the A6 south of Bakewell on the B5056 to Ashbourne. In 3½ miles, Robin Hood's Stride and Cratcliffe Tor, a prominent gritstone crag, are clearly seen to the right of the road. Stop immediately before a left hand bend, where a minor road joins on the right, and directly below the crags. Park where it is unlikely to cause obstruction. (G.R. 228618).*

ROUTE

1. *Where the minor road bends left, take the track to the right leading up towards Cratcliffe Tor. Leave this where it bends right towards cottages and continue straight up by the wall on the left to the gap between the Tor and the Stride. A footpath to the right leads in 250 metres to Hermit's Cave, situated at the foot of the crag. Retrace your steps to the gap.*

2. *Continue through an open gateway, across two fields with stiles, to a minor road. Cross this and follow the track to the farm at Castle Ring. Bypass it on the left, then bear right to a stile with yellow markings. Continue across and down the steep embankment to a stile and a track which forks. Take the left fork and follow this to where it ends in a field.*

3. *Turn right and head down through fields with stiles, using the church tower at Youlgreave as your guide. In ½ mile the footpath joins a minor road.*

4. *Turn right, cross a bridge, then left into Bradford Dale. (Shortly, a footpath to the right leads up into Youlgreave. Rejoin the route at the first footbridge).*

5. *Follow the footpath to a footbridge. Cross it and continue, now on the left bank, passing a bridge on the way, to a second bridge where the path is forced once more over the river.*

6. *After crossing the bridge turn left and continue along the right bank, over a footbridge, then up a wooden staircase.*

7. *Turn right, and stay on the left bank. Continue to a fork in the footpath.*

8. *Take the right fork, which leads more or less straight ahead to a stile. Continue ascending in the same direction to a farm and caravan site (Hopping Farm). Go through the farm to a stile directly ahead. Continue straight on up the steepening hill following the wall on the left.*

9 *At the top of the field go through a stile and left to another. Turn right here and continue up the steep slope, crossing a minor road, to a stone stile in a wall running along the crest of the hill.*

10. *Head for the top corner of a plantation (Bleakley), passing through a stile, to an open gateway. Continue in the same direction through another open gateway and on to a stile.*

11. *Bear right to a stile and continue in the same direction to an obscure stile about half way along the wall opposite.*

12. *Cross it and walk by the wall on the right, passing what should be a stile in 150 metres, to an open gateway. Pass through this and bear right across the field to another open gateway. Continue in the same general direction to the corner of Tomlinson Wood and a third open gateway. Keeping to the right edge of the wood, follow it until it bends left, then bear right to a well marked stile.*

13. *Head for a point half way between the small wood on the left and a farm to the right until a track is met.*

14. *Turn left along the track, cross a minor road, and continue down another track to where it bends to the right.*

15. *Turn left and follow the rough track to Robin Hood's Stride and 'the gap'. Return along the first section of the route.*

ACCESS BY BUS

To Robin Hood's Stride from Chesterfield, Bakewell & Matlock (Silver Service), weekdays only.

To Youlgreave from Chesterfield & Bakewell (Silver Service), daily.

With all the history and other diversions now behind you, the way back to the Stride requires that the party partakes in a new game, "Find-the-Stile", since the footpath is largely non-existent!

Should you get chance to raise your eyes above the level of the next wall, look out for the curlew, whose distinctive call betrays their presence, as well as meadow pipit, lapwing and wheatears with their eye-catching white rumps.

Refreshments Bull's Head at Youlgreave. Children admitted, benches and tables in courtyard, coffee and lunches available.

Farmyard Inn, Youlgreave. Children admitted, benches and tables across road from pub, tea, coffee, lunches available.

George Hotel, Youlgreave. Children admitted, no outside drinking facilities, tea, coffee and lunches available.

Meadow Cottage Cafe and tea garden by the first footbridge in Bradford Dale.

Route 11

5½ miles

(Shorter variation 4 miles)

Chee Dale

Outline

Millersdale ~ Priestcliffe ~ Blackwell ~ Chee Dale ~ Millersdale

Summary   Probably the most scenically interesting and adventurous walk in this guide, offering a contrast between the gentle rolling pastures of the limestone plateau and a wooded gorge with huge cliffs and a winding river. The walk begins by ascending a fairly steep footpath out of Millersdale through a Nature Reserve but is rewarded by excellent views of Monk's Dale to the northwest, and lower Chee Dale to the west. Once on the plateau, a little used footpath is followed through meadows. A minor road is then taken through the hamlets of Priestcliffe and Blackwell, which is left by a cart-track. A well-stiled footpath leads down to the disused railway track which cuts through the dale. The track is soon forsaken, however, for a more adventurous route by the river's edge. The footpath, whilst interesting in dry conditions, can be difficult in or after wet weather. It can be very slippery and also uses stepping stones which may be under water, though usually by not more than a few inches. Having passed through some of the most spectacular gorge scenery in these parts, the short section of the Monsal Trail over the Millersdale viaduct provides a fitting conclusion to the walk.

Attractions   The most strenuous section of the walk, the ascent out of Millersdale, comes right at the beginning and is soon over with. On the top side of the disused railway track, now part of the Monsal Trail, the footpath passes through a Nature Reserve. Whilst interesting species of wild flower are protected here, the butterfly spotter would have a field day.

   After the initial, sharp ascent, the route traces a gently undulating line through peaceful meadows where a horse-drawn cart would not seem out of place, then takes to country lanes through the old hamlets of Priestcliffe and Blackwell, the latter possessing two campsites and a farm shop open in season.

   The Monsal Trail, regained at the top of Chee Dale, is a masterpiece of railway engineering constructed in the mid 19th century by the Midland Railway. Now a disused track, nature is claiming it back as its own, forcing it to blend into the natural surroundings. To the right of the track is the impressive Plum Buttress, a huge limestone cliff with a notorious climb, Surplomb, forcing its way up the overhanging top section.

   Once down in the dale, the walk by the river is an adventure in itself. Virtually inescapable, the footpath hugs the narrow river bank, which in

continued on page 52

Route 11

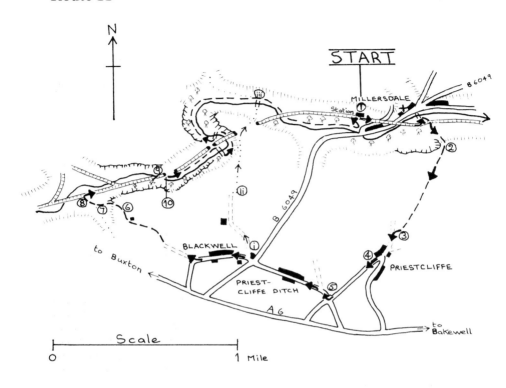

MARSH MARIGOLD
Yellow March-August

50

Route 11
Chee Dale 5½ miles

(Shorter variation 4 miles)

START   *Park at Millersdale Station (G.R. 138734), which is now a Peak Warden's base with toilets and information posters. To get to the station carpark, take the road signposted to Wormhill. After passing under a railway bridge, turn left.*

ROUTE
1. *From the carpark, follow the disused railway track over the viaduct. Soon after crossing the viaduct a footpath coming up from Millersdale crosses the track. Turn right here and follow the footpath through a Nature Reserve, then steeply uphill on the left of an old quarry to a stile at the top.*
2. *Head for the far corner of the field and a stile and continue in the same direction along a well-stiled footpath with way-markings to a track.*
3. *Turn left into Priestcliffe. The track soon joins a minor road at a sharp bend.*
4. *Bear right and follow the road up to a crossroads.*
5. *Turn right and continue downhill through Priestcliffe Ditch to a main road. Cross it and follow the lane through Blackwell to a sharp left hand bend, with a campsite on the right. Leave the road and go straight on, over a stile by a gate, then along an overgrown track. Follow it to its end and a stile. Continue straight on to another stile, then bear left towards a ruined barn. Pass it on the left and head for the bottom left corner of the field.*
6. *Turn left at a stile and continue to another straight ahead. Cross this and keep to the wall on the left. Where it forms a corner, bear slightly right to zigzag down a steep slope to a wooden stile.*
7. *Turn right and follow the footpath down to the disused railway track, access being on the left of the bridge.*
8. *Turn right and follow the track to within 100 metres of the tunnel, where a viaduct carries it over the river.*
9. *At the far side of the viaduct, on the left, descend the steps leading down and under it to a footpath by the river.*
10. *Turn left. Follow the footpath downstream, making a short diversion to the right bank via footbridges. In just over 2 miles the footpath ends at a gate, and a path (signposted), doubles back upwards to the left to the Monsal Trail and the carpark.*

SHORTER VARIATION

As for 1 to 5 above as far as Blackwell, then:

i. *Take the first metalled road to the right, leading to Blackwell Hall Farm. Continue past the farm along a track and follow it to its end.*

ii. *Turn right, then left, keeping close to the wall on the left. Continue over two stiles, then bear right down a steep slope to a footbridge and the river.*

iii. *Cross it, turn right and continue along the riverside footpath to a gate. Continue as for 10 & 11 above)*

ACCESS BY BUS

To Millersdale from Stoke, Buxton & Sheffeld (Trent/Potteries), weekdays only.

---

two places disappears altogether, further progress being made possible by stepping stones. These can be under water and call for initiative from the larger members of the party.

As if this was not enough, in summer giant rhubarb-like butterbur and lurking nettles try to impede progress but, fortunately, over only short sections. On the subject of riverside plants, Chee Dale provides an ideal habitat for a wide range of wild flowers, including water forget-me-not, meadowsweet and the bright yellow monkey flower.

Just before the gorge opens out into a wider valley, it bends in a horseshoe shape around Chee Tor. Here, the river has cut through over 200 feet of rock, leaving sheer cliffs on both sides of the gorge. Though there are now climbs of a much higher standard, the classic route is the high level traverse of the cliff on the opposite side of the river to the footpath. In summer, climbers can be seen queuing along the route.

Once through this section of the dale, the walk becomes a pleasant stroll by the stream. If the mood takes you or the offspring, there are several good, safe spots for picnicking, paddling and watching riverside birds such as dipper, grey wagtail and kingfisher (if you happen to be looking in the right direction when it darts past).

By taking the Monsal Trail back over the viaduct, a suitably spectacular situation high above the road through Millersdale completes the walk in style.

Refreshments   Campsite farm shop at Blackwell.

Angler's Rest at Millersdale. Children admitted, seats and walls for outside drinkers, coffee and bar snacks available.

Route 12

Monk's Dale and Tideswell Dale

Outline

Tideswell ~ Monk's Dale ~ Millersdale ~ Tideswell Dale ~ Tideswell.

Summary Starting and finishing at Tideswell, a busy market village since the 13th century, the walk takes two dales complete, Monk's Dale and Tideswell Dale, as well as a short section of Miller's Dale. From Tideswell, a footpath through meadows, then a minor road, lead to the head of Monk's Dale. The walk through the dale can be difficult underfoot in wet conditions, when all effort and concentration would be spent looking down at the ground ahead rather than appreciating the wild and unspoiled surroundings. On reaching Millersdale, the Monsal Trail is followed for ½ mile, from which the impressive Raven's Tor can be glimpsed, then an easy footpath through Tideswell Dale (now a Nature Trail) then a farm track, lead back into the village.

Attractions For the budding botanist, Monk's Dale is a paradise, with over a hundred recorded species of wild flower. Amongst the scree by the side of the footpath, which incidentally, is quite rich in fossils, you may come across bloody crane's-bill, with its startling deep crimson coloured flowers, as well as the dark red helleborine. The yellow rock rose can be seen on the more open grassy sections. Part of the Derbyshire Dales Nature Reserve, and virtually untouched by man or his livestock, the dale is one of the wildest in the National Park, and of more than a passing interest to anyone with a keen eye for wildlife.

At Ravenstor, it can be fun watching the antics of climbers making their way up, down or across the overhanging cliff face. On an off day, when the crag is devoid of such traffic, it is still worth stopping to play at "Spot the Route". By careful scrutiny of the placements of slings, various ironmongery, and those tell-tale chalk marks, it is possible to deduce where many of the lines are.

Tideswell Dale provides a pleasant saunter with one or two interesting looking caves-cum-mines by the footpath. Pamphlets covering the Nature Trail are available at the Information Centre at the top of the dale but would have to be collected before starting the walk or on a previous visit to the area.

continued on page 56

53

Route 12

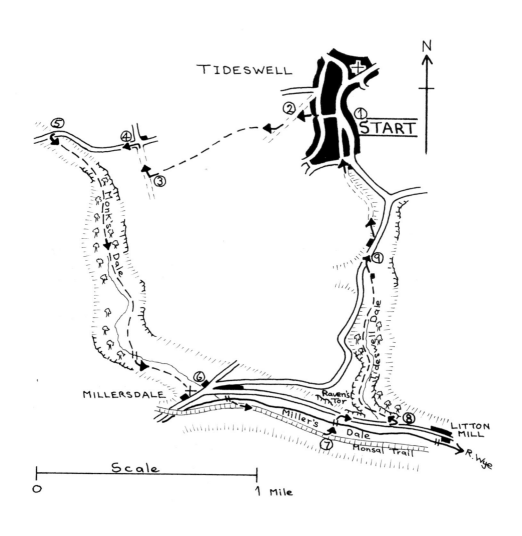

TIDESWELL

START

N

Monk's Dale

MILLERSDALE

Raven's Tor

Miller's Dale

Monsal Trail

LITTON MILL

R. Wye

Tideswell Dale

Scale

0   1 Mile

Route 12

Monk's Dale and Tideswell Dale   5½ miles

START *At Cherry Tree Square in Tideswell, about 200 metres down from the church on the main road through the village. (G.R. 153755).*

ROUTE

1. *Go up Sunny Bank Lane to the T-junction at the top. Go straight across to a stile opposite and continue in the same direction along a well-stiled footpath to where it joins a track.*

2. *Turn left. In about 150 metres turn right at a stile and continue along a footpath through meadows to a track. Stiles point the way although one or two are not so obvious at first glance.*

3. *Turn right and follow the track to a minor road.*

4. *Turn left and continue along the road down into the dale. Monk's Dale is to the left and Peter Dale to the right.*

5. *Enter Monk's Dale and take the obvious rocky footpath running parallel to the stream (often dry). About a mile downsteam the footpath ascends the left side of the valley before descending to a footbridge. Cross this and continue down to the church at Millersdale.*

6. *Cross the main road to join the minor road which passes in front of the Angler's Rest. Turn right just beyond the water-wheel to cross the river by a footbridge. Continue up to the Monsal Trail. Turn left and follow the trail to the first exit on the left, signposted "Youth Hostel".*

7. *Leave the trail at this point and recross the river at a second footbridge to rejoin the road from Millersdale to Litton Mill. (Raven's Tor is 200 metres to the left and out of sight). Turn right and walk along the road for ¼ mile to where Tideswell Dale joins Miller's Dale on the left.*

8. *Turn left here and follow the footpath up the dale to the Information Centre. Continue to the road.*

9. *Turn right and follow the road to a stile on the left immediately past the sewage works. Cross the stile and bear right up to a track. Follow this back into Tideswell.*

ACCESS BY BUS

To Tideswell from Chesterfield & Bakewell (Silver Service and East Midland), summer Sundays and Bank Holidays only, and from Stoke, Buxton and Sheffield (Trent/Potteries), weekdays only.

Tideswell, its name derived from the Saxon Tidi's waelle, meaning Tidi's spring, is an ancient settlement. In the 13th century it was transformed into a busy market village, becoming the centre of the lead and wool trade in this area. The church is the biggest and perhaps finest in the Peak District. Built between 1320 and 1380, it undoubtedly testifies to the importance of the village in the 14th century.

Refreshments Angler's Rest Inn, at Millersdale. Children admitted, seats and walls for outside drinkers, coffee and bar snacks available.

George Inn, Tideswell. Children admitted, facilities for outside drinking, tea, coffee and food available.

Cafe at Tideswell.

THE WYE AT LITTON MILL

56

Miller's Dale

Outline
Litton Mill ~ Cressbrook ~ Monsal Head ~ Brushfield ~ Litton Mill.

Summary A concessionary footpath alongside the River Wye is followed through the impressive gorge of Water-cum-Jolly to Cressbrook. From here, a short section of road-walking leads to a footpath which ascends quite steeply to Monsal Head, where the party can rest and take refreshments. A descent to the Monsal Viaduct follows, at the far side of which the route breaks off to ascend the opposite side of the valley. Once at the top, the hard work is over and a level track, from which there are excellent views of Monsal Dale, is followed to the tiny hamlet of Brushfield. The track is forsaken for a footpath a little further on which leads across and down into Miller's Dale, crossing the Monsal Trail and River Wye before arriving back at Litton Mill.

Attractions Water-cum-Jolly is a true gorge with impressive cliffs, a river, and a mill-pond which is in keeping with its surroundings. Amongst the reeds coot and moorhen dabble about, and it is not uncommon to sight a kingfisher in these parts. Dabbling about on the overhanging limestone buttresses members of the human species are often seen.

The mill at Cressbrook, established by Sir Richard Arkwright for cotton spinning in 1783, was water powered, as was Litton Mill. Under the management, then ownership, of William Newton, the apprentices were reasonably well treated. Just before leaving the dale, on the left, and by the mill-race, is the apprentice house, resembling a miniature castle. Litton Mill, built by Ellis Needham in 1782, was equally well known for the cruelty of its owner towards his pauper apprentices. So many died as a result of their ill treatment that, to avoid embarrassment, burials were equally split between the graveyards of Tideswell and Taddington Churches.

Brushfield, a tiny and attractive cluster of farm buildings, has some surprises in store. Any combination of goats, sheep, hens and cats, not to mention a peacock, may be seen roaming about the place. On the right is a large cage used for breeding budgerigars and parakeets or similar. All in all, a quaint little menagerie.

The footpath across to Miller's Dale passes through old lead mine workings, evidenced by the depressions in the surface. Here, wild flowers

continued on page 60

57

Route 13

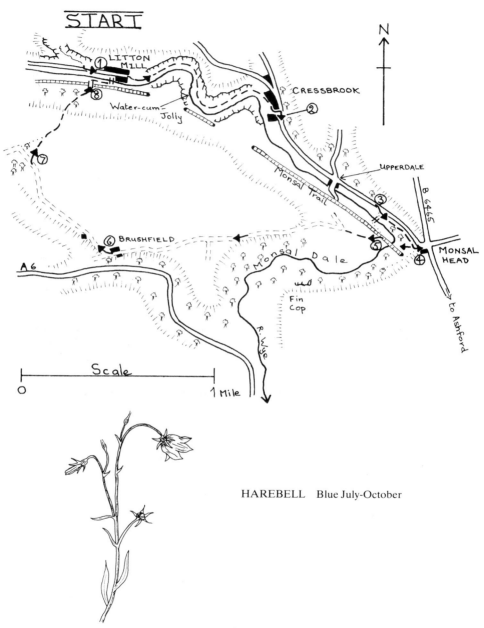

START

LITTON MILL ①

⑧

Water-cum-Jolly

CRESSBROOK

②

N

UPPERDALE

⑦

Monsal Trail

③

B 6465

Monsal Dale

⑥ BRUSHFIELD

A 6

Fin Cop

⑤

④ MONSAL HEAD

R. Wye

to Ashford

Scale

0   1 Mile

HAREBELL   Blue July-October

Route 13
Miller's Dale

6 miles

START   *From Millersdale, which lies 2 miles south of Tideswell on the B6049, take the road passing in front of the Angler's Rest for 1 mile to an obvious car parking space at the foot of Tideswell Dale and immediately before Litton Mill. (G.R. 155732)*

ROUTE
1. *Walk along the road to Litton Mill. Continue straight through the mill itself and into Water-cum-Jolly. The footpath leaves the river bank through another mill yard at Cressbrook.*
2. *Turn right at the road and follow it, passing Upperdale en route, to where it begins to climb.*
3. *At this point, either continue along the road up to Monsal Head, or, better, bear right to take the footpath running parallel to the road and leading to the same point.*
4. *From the viewpoint at Monsal Head, regain the footpath and follow the well signposted route down on to the viaduct.*
5. *On the far side of this, turn left at a gate and fork right up a walled footpath. Where it meets up with a track, continue in the same direction along this up the hill. Keep on the track and continue to Brushfield (1¼ miles).*
6. *On leaving the hamlet, turn right at a track and follow this to a farm. Pass it on the right and continue along the track for ½ mile as far as a wood on the left.*
7. *Turn right at a stile opposite the wood and continue through fields with stiles. When the footpath begins to descend, it bears right to an old footbridge over the Monsal Trail.*
8. *Turn right after the bridge and, keeping to the left of a wall, descend to a footbridge and cross over into Litton Mill. Turn left to finish.*

ACCESS BY BUS

To Monsal Head only, from Chesterfield, Buxton & Macclesfield (East Midland/Crossville), Saturdays, Sundays and Bank Holidays, and from Bakewell (Andrews), Monday to Friday only.

grow in abundance. As one descends towards Litton Mill an ideal picnic spot is reached from which Water-cum-Jolly can be glimpsed.

Refreshments Monsal Head Hotel. Children admitted, beer garden, tea, coffee and lunches available.

Monsal Head Cafe.

Upperdale Farm Cafe.

VILLAGE CROSS, LITTON

Route 14

(Shorter variation 3 miles)

Cressbrook Dale and Litton

Outline

Wardlow Mires ~ Cressbrook Dale ~ Litton ~ Wardlow Mires.

Summary The walk down the dale is along a well-trodden footpath, though it tends to be quieter than other dales. The first part is open and treeless but soon closes in to become a heavily wooded and steep-sided valley. The footpath out of the valley bottom degenerates into a scramble for the last 200 feet, and is followed by a virtually untrodden path, a little awkward underfoot, along the top of a wood for ¼ mile, before breaking out into the open across fields to Litton. The last section follows a road for ½ mile, returning across fields to the start. The shorter variation misses out the wooded part of the dale and takes a footpath direct to Litton via Tansley Dale.

Attractions In the upper part of the dale is Peter's Stone, a limestone knoll resembling a mountain in miniature and simply asking to be conquered. In the gap between the knoll and the valley side the screes are rich in fossils, as well as crickets, grasshoppers and snails.

Further on, there is evidence of old mine workings, and it is worth rummaging around in the discarded debris to try to identify the minerals which may have been extracted.

The wooded part of the dale, with its huge, white limestone cliff, Raven Crag, is wild and unspoilt, and seems almost unchanged since prehistoric times. A haven for shy woodland birds, look out for warblers, the spotted flycatcher, redstart and green woodpecker, the latter usually heard rather than seen. Also along this section of the dale, the plant spotter might be interested to know that cowslips and early purple orchids abound, and wooded anemones are also quite common hereabouts.

Whilst much of the footpath in the dale is of the rough and ready kind, the scramble through the wood up the last 200 feet of the valley side, followed by a partially overgrown footpath trapped between a wall and the top of the wood, provide scope for the young pioneer.

Once out of the dale, the character of the walk changes abruptly. Looking across towards Litton, the eye is met with a spectacle only seen in these parts; walls, miles of them, forming an intricate network of field strips, some only a few metres wide, and testifying to a way of living and farming belonging to a bygone age.

continued on page 64

61

Route 14

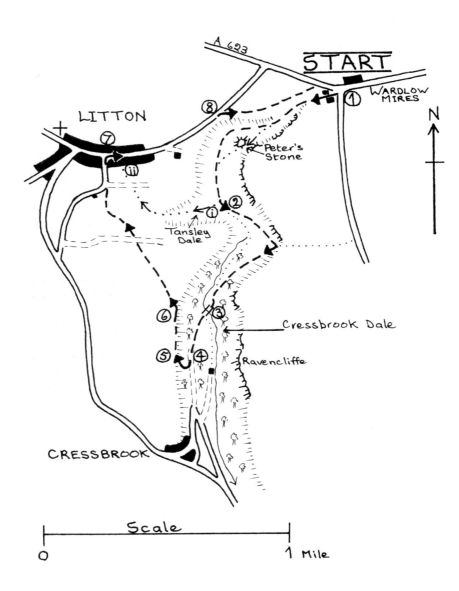

Scale

0   1 Mile

Route 14
Cressbrook Dale and Litton

4½ miles

(Shorter variation 3 miles)

START   *Park opposite the Three Stags Head at Wardlow Mires on the A623. (G.R. 182756).*

ROUTE

1. *The footpath begins at a gate between a cottage and an outbuilding on the far side of the T-junction 100 metres from the pub. Keep to the valley bottom, passing beneath Peter's Stone, a prominent limestone knoll. In just under a mile, the path is joined by another at a stile on the right, and a well-trodden footpath forks left up the hillside.*

2. *The public right of way takes this left fork to a point near the top, then a right fork leads back down the slope to the stream and a footbridge. (A footpath, which is the natural continuation of the one followed from Wardlow Mires, does exist. It clings to the left bank of the often dry stream-bed and arrives at the very same footbridge.)*

3. *Cross the footbridge and ascend the slope, keeping to the left of a wall and wood. The footpath becomes a wider track where it levels out. Continue along this to where it enters woods.*

4. *A few metres into the wood, and on the right, a footpath, signposted Litton, permits a continuation of the ascent out of the valley. Ignore any footpaths which begin to contour. Instead, scramble up steeply amongst the trees and tree-roots, bearing only slightly right.*

5. *At the top, turn right and follow the narrow footpath, awkward in parts with a steep slope hidden by foliage on the right.*

6. *In ¼ mile, turn left at a stile. Bear right, and continue through fields with stiles to a track. Cross the track to a stile opposite and continue in the same direction through more fields with stiles to a minor road. Follow this to a junction in the village.*

7. *Turn right (left for the Red Lion), and walk along the road for ½ mile to a stile on the right.*

8. *Turn right here and continue direct to Wardlow Mires, keeping above the valley.*

Shorter Variation   As for 1 above, then:

i. *Turn right at the stile, follow the footpath up through the tiny Tansley Dale and bear right near its end to a track. Turn left and in a few metres climb a stone stile on the right. Continue into the village.*

ii. *Turn right and continue as for 7 & 8 above.*

ACCESS BY BUS

To 'Three Stags Head', Wardlow Mires, from Chesterfield (Silver Service), summer Sundays and Bank Holidays only.

Litton, an interesting old village with almost as many farm buildings as houses, forms the hub of this ancient field system. At the centre of the village is the green with its market cross. Unlike the stocks at Eyam, those at Litton are anything but ancient, having been erected only a few years ago for a village fete.

Refreshments   Red Lion at Litton. Children admitted for bar lunches. Faces village green for outside drinking.

Three Stags Head at Wardlow Mires.

HOB'S HOUSE

Monsal Dale and Brushfield Hough

Outline

White Lodge ~ Brushfield Hough ~ Monsal Head ~ White Lodge.

Summary   The walk begins at the foot of Monsal Dale but straightaway climbs out of the valley by a footpath winding up through woods, and ending up at the farm at Brushfield Hough, from which there is a fine view of the dale. A track along the crest of the valley side is then taken as far as the Monsal Trail and viaduct, from which a short, steep footpath leads up to the viewpoint and refreshments at Monsal Head. The rest is downhill, and along well-trodden footpaths, first through a wood, then alongside the river and back to the start.

Attractions   The steep path at the start of the walk gets the hard work over with straightaway, when the youngsters are boiling with that initial surge of enthusiasm. For older members of the party, there are plenty of excuses to stop and ponder over the wildlife in the ash woods, taking special note of the wild flowers by the side of the footpath.

From the old farm at Brushfield Hough, picturesque in itself, there is a fine view of the dale from a vantage point rarely seen by visitors to the area, and opposite is the impressive hill, Fin Cop, once an Iron Age fort. Looking across at the hillside, it is easy to make out the course of ancient footpaths that once zig-zagged down to the river, their main function probably for fetching water.

The walk along the former railway viaduct provides thrills, but spitting and throwing stones on to unsuspecting persons or ducks below should be discouraged. The railway enthusiast may be interested to know that the viaduct once carried the Midland railway across the River Wye, linking Buxton with Matlock.

The view from Monsal Head is certainly one of the finest in the Peak District, with a pub, a cafe, and, usually, an ice-cream van conveniently situated at the same spot, thereby catering for all tastes.

Hob's House is a worthy deviation with a lot of interest for young and old alike. Bearing no resemblance to a house, it is a limestone knoll cut off from the hillside and riddled with deep clefts which may be the remnants of caves whose roofs have collapsed. 3000 years ago, in the Bronze Age, the place was a burial site, where individual tombs were erected over some of the rock cavities. Whilst there is ample scope for exploring, scrambling, hide and seek etc., the screes are a fossil paradise.

continued on page 68

Route 15

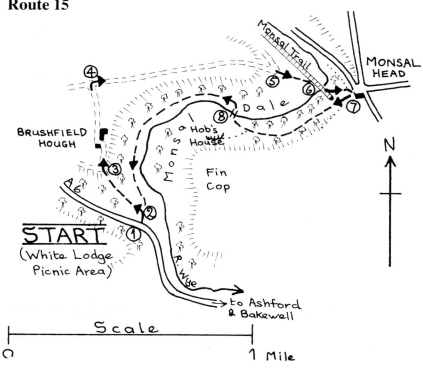

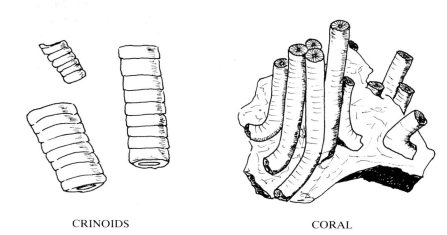

CRINOIDS   CORAL

Route 15

Monsal Dale and Brushfield Hough

3 miles

START   *At White Lodge car park and picnic area, 2 miles west of Ashford-in-the-Water on the A6. (G.R. 171706).*

ROUTE

1. *From the car park, cross the main road to enter Monsal Dale.*
2. *A few metres past the wooden stile turn left (signposted Brushfield) and follow the winding and ascending footpath through woods to a stile and track at the top of the hill.*
3. *Turn right and continue along the track to the farm at Brushfield Hough. Keep to the arrowed path through the farm, leaving it by the track behind the long barn. Continue to where it joins another track.*
4. *Turn right and follow this for ⅓ mile, first on the level, then as it descends, to where it bends sharp left.*
5. *Leave the track and continue straight on along a walled footpath, vague and overgrown in parts, and down on to the Monsal viaduct.*
6. *Turn right and cross the viaduct, then go left at the far side and ascend the steep path to Monsal Head.*
7. *Go back through the stile by the cafe and continue straight down the major footpath through woods to the river and a footbridge. (150 metres after the descent becomes noticeably steeper, a footpath to the left and contouring the hillside leads to Hob's House. Return to the main footpath to continue.)*
8. *Cross the footbridge, turn left and follow the footpath by the river back to the start.*

ACCESS BY BUS

To Monsal Dale from Chesterfield, Bakewell, Buxton & Macclesfield (East Midland/Crosville), weekends and public holidays.

No hammers or chisels are necessary. Previous demolition squads have left a sufficient supply of samples for ready identification. If you are carrying a torch, an obvious cave can be explored for 20 metres or so.

The dale, being wide and flat, is much like a park, with large areas of natural lawn interrupted by trees and shrubs. The river has an impressive weir with a waterfall beneath which the done thing on a warm day is to paddle and splash about. Along the quieter stretches, coot and moorhen can be seen, whereas mallard are more attracted to the busier spots in the hope of being offered morsels from the packed lunch. Dipper are quite common by the river's edge, as are grey wagtail, and a more trained eye should spot one or two common sandpiper as well as the odd bullfinch. There are reputed to be a pair of kingfishers to every mile along the River Wye. Unless you are very lucky, you will see neither of them over this stretch of river. Though wild flowers abound in the dale, in the lower reaches look out in particular for the yellow monkey flower.

Refreshments Monsal Head Hotel. Children admitted, beer garden, tea, coffee and lunches available.

Monsal Head Cafe.

SHEEPWASH BRIDGE

68

Route 16

5½ miles

(Shorter variation 4½ miles)

Deep Dale, Sheldon and Great Shacklow Wood

Outline   White Lodge (Picnic Area) ~ Deep Dale ~ Sheldon ~ Ashford ~ White Lodge.

Summary   A delightful walk taking in a quiet dale, an attractive little village, and a stretch of wild, mixed woodland. The route takes a footpath through Deep Dale before striking out up the valley side and into Sheldon. The village is left by a footpath that leads back down to the Wye Valley and to Ashford-in-the-Water. The way back is along a well-trodden but nevertheless interesting path which at first clings to the river's edge, but then ascends sharply into Great Shacklow Wood, finally descending again to the Picnic Area.

Attractions   Not far from the Picnic Area, to the right of the footpath and well camouflaged, is a shallow cave which was used by Middle Stone Age people as a rock shelter between 10,000 and 8,000 years ago. Here, over 500 tools made from flint and chert were discovered on excavation of the cave floor. These included scrapers, microliths, knives and awls. Evidently, the community must have been toolmakers, quarrying the nearby screes for chert, a black flintlike rock which, when split, leaves razor sharp edges.

On approaching Sheldon the chimney and derelict buildings of Magpie Mine can be clearly seen across the fields. Well worth a visit, arrangements can be made to view the surface workings by contacting the Mining Museum at Matlock Bath. The "sough" which drains the mine of water emerges by the footpath on the way back from Ashford.

Sheldon, now an almost forgotten village, especially since the old Inn became a private residence, was an important farming and mining community for several hundred years. Entered in the Domesday Book as "Schelhadun", the name suggests that the village was a settlement long before the Norman Conquest.

On entering Ashford, the old packhorse bridge known as Sheepwash Bridge is crossed. Presumably, as the sheep entered the village on market day they were made to wade through the river by the bridge to wash off parasites. Ashford, now a relatively quiet back-water, in the past vied with Bakewell as a market village, and in the 17th century as many as 300 packhorses passed through each week. On the western entrance to the village black 'marble' - a dark stained limestone -was mined. Opened in

continued on page 72

Route 16

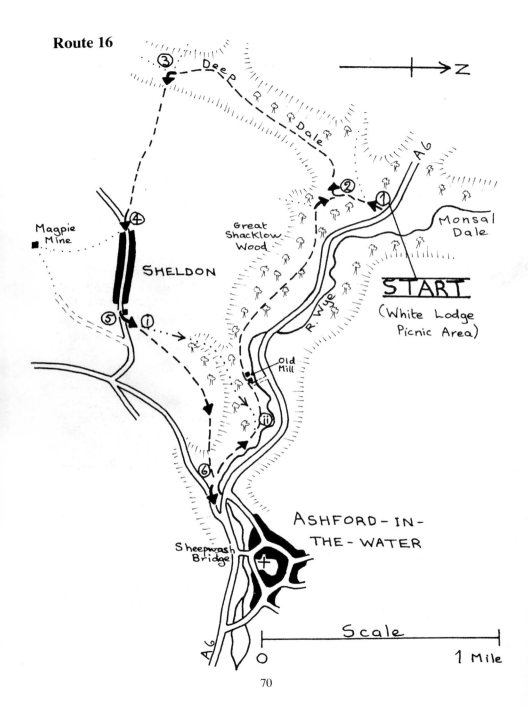

Route 16

Deep Dale, Sheldon and Great Shacklow Wood 5½ miles

(Shorter variation 4½ miles)

START *At White Lodge Picnic Area at the foot of Monsal Dale and 2 miles west of Ashford-in-the-Water along the A6. (G.R. 171706).*

ROUTE

1. *Leave the Picnic Area by the stile on the south side. Follow the winding footpath, cross another stile, and continue to a signpost, where the path forks.*

2. *Take the right fork and follow the footpath into Deep Dale. Continue for a mile to where a wall blocks the way forward. A small gate on the right permits further progress up the dale but only go as far as the stile on the left in 60 metres.*

3. *Cross it and go straight up the valley side to a stile at the top. Continue in the same direction, keeping close to the wall on the left, passing through several gates. Where the wall turns sharp left, bear slightly left to a stile, then continue as before to reach a minor road at a stile by a gate.*

4. *Turn left and follow the road into and through Sheldon, at the far side of which the road dips into a gully.*

5. *Turn left at a stile. The footpath forks. Take the higher level path to the right and follow this down through fields with stiles, bearing right where the ground steepens. When the line of the footpath becomes vague, head for Ashford, which is clearly visible from this point. The path joins the riverside footpath along the Wye. The way back is to the left. (For Ashford, turn right, continue over a stile, then left to the main road. Turn right and take the first bridge over the river, which is Sheepwash Bridge, and so into the village. Retrace your steps.)*

6. *Follow the riverside footpath, passing behind the old mill, and continue along this as it climbs into Great Shacklow Wood. A stile is crossed before the path descends once more to the valley and the start.*

SHORTER VARIATION

As for 1 to 4 above then:

i. *After turning left at the stile (as for 5 above), take the footpath heading straight down the gully into the woods. Follow it to the river at the bottom.*

ii. *Turn left and continue as for 6 above.*

ACCESS BY BUS Same as for Route 15.

the mid 18th century, with accompanying mill, the mine supplied stone which was cut and polished for use in ornamental work. Examples of this can be seen at Chatsworth House, where it was used for interior decoration.

On the walk back alongside the River Wye the old mill with its rusting metal water-wheels provides interest. Apparently, one of the wheels was used to pump water up to Sheldon before mains water was laid.

Further on, the footpath climbs into Great Shacklow Wood, with its tall trees and dense undergrowth. Strangely, although the footpath is never more than 300 metres from the main road, one has the impression of being in a remote forest. Though brown bears are not so common in these parts, a walk through the wood on a moonlit night would most likely conjure them from the imagination. If field glasses are carried, keep an eye out for tree-creepers as well as wood warblers, tits and various other small woodland birds.

Refreshments   The Bull's Head at Ashford. Children admitted, outside seating, tea, coffee and bar lunches available.

The Devonshire Arms at Ashford. Children admitted, beer garden, tea, coffee and bar lunches available.

Cafe at Ashford.

THE WYE AT ASHFORD

Appendices

ROUTES IN ORDER OF DIFFICULTY

Starting with the easiest:

Route 14 - *Cressbrook Dale and Litton (shorter variation)*
Route 7 - *Lathkill Dale, upper section*
Route 9 - *Lathkill Dale, lower section*
Route 15 - *Monsal Dale and Brushfield Hough*
Route 11 - *Chee Dale (shorter variation)*
Route 1 - *Thor's Cave and Ossom's Hill*
Route 14 - *Cressbrook Dale and Litton*
Route 8 - *Lathkill Dale, middle section*
Route 16 - *Deep Dale (shorter variation)*
Route 6 - *Longnor and Earl Sterndale*
Route 12 - *Monk's Dale and Tideswell Dale*
Route 5 - *Beresford Dale and Biggin Dale*
Route 4 - *Wolfscote Dale and Narrow Dale (via stepping stones)*
Route 13 - *Miller's Dale*
Route 16 - *Deep Dale*
Route 3 - *Upper Dove Dale and Hall Dale*
Route 10 - *Harthill Moor and Bradford Dale*
Route 4 - *Wolfscote Dale and Narrow Dale (via footbridge)*
Route 11 - *Chee Dale*
Route 2 - *Dove Dale*

BUS OPERATORS TO AND WITHIN THE WHITE PEAK (applicable to walks)

Andrews of Tideswell .... Tel. Buxton 871222
Crosville Motor Services Ltd. .... Tel. Macclesfield 28855
East Midland Motor Services Ltd. .... Tel. Chesterfield 75432
Potteries Motor Traction Co. Ltd. .... Tel. Stoke 48811
Silver Service Group .... Tel. Baslow 2246
South Yorkshire Transport .... Tel. Sheffield 78688
Trent Motor Traction Co. Ltd. .... Tel. Derby 372078
Ashbourne 42360   Buxton 3098   Matlock 2013
W N Warrington ....Tel. Thorpe Cloud 204

CYCLE HIRE CENTRES

Ashbourne — Mapleton Road. Tel. Ashbourne 43156
Tissington — the building adjacent to the village pond. Tel. Parwich 244
Middleton Top — 4½ miles south of Matlock half way between Middleton and Wirksworth off the B5023, at a picnic site on the High Peak Trail. Tel. Wirksworth 3204
Hartington — 2 The Market Place. Tel. Hartington 459 or Ashbourne 42629
Parsley Hay — 2 miles south of Monyash and just off the A515 Buxton to Ashbourne, at a picnic site on the High Peak Trail. Tel. Hartington 493
Monsal Head — adjacent to the Monsal Head Hotel on the B6465 1½ miles N.W. of Ashford-in-the-Water. — Tel. Gt. Longstone 505 or Tideswell 871679
Derwent — Fairholmes Picnic Site, below the Derwent Dam, 2 miles north of Ashopton Viaduct (A57-Snake Pass). Tel. 0433-51261

Waterhouses — Waterhouses Station Car Park. Situated near the southern end of the Manifold Track. Tel. 05386-609

Hayfield — Hayfield Station Picnic Site on the Sett Valley Trail, just off the A624 Chapel to Glossop road. Tel. 0663-46222

Lyme Park — Lyme Park National Trust Country Park, Disley. Tel. 06632-2023

Bollington — By the Peak and Plains Discovery Centre, Grimshaw Lane, Bollington, on the Middlewood Way and Cheshire Cycle Way. Tel. 0625-72681

NATURE TRAILS

Black Rocks Trail — ½ mile south of Cromford off the B5036, and starting at the Black Rocks Picnic Area.

Errwood Hall Trail — Goyt Valley. Turn off the A5002 2 miles N.W. of Buxton. The trail starts at a Picnic area.

Ilam Nature Trail — in the grounds of Ilam Hall, Ilam.

Padley and Longshaw Nature Trail — starts at Longshaw Lodge, just off the A625 between Sheffield and Hathersage.

Sett Valley Trail — starts at Hayfield Station Picnic site, just off the A624 Chapel to Glossop road.

Lyme Park Nature Trail — Lyme Park, Disley.

Tideswell Dale Trail — starts at a Picnic Area 1 mile south of Tideswell.

PICNIC PLACES

Although there are innumerable spots which could be mentioned, the few that are listed below are those that are both easily accessible and which provide a child with plenty of scope for exploration and inventive play. They are not, as are official picnic sites, provided with litter bins, toilets and tables, and anyone using these places should obey the Country Code.

Biggin Dale (G.R. 145587)   At the fork in the dale, ½ mile south of Dale End (see Route 5), is an attractive, sheltered and grassy area safe for younger children to play and explore, with the more interesting lower part of the dale near at hand to satisfy the needs of older children. This area is also a Nature Reserve.

Robin Hood's Stride (G.R. 226623)   (See Route 10) The whole section from the Stride to, and including, Cratcliffe Tor provides plenty of scope for picnicking, exploring, weaselling beneath boulders, hide and seek, and much more. A word of caution, however! Any wanderings in the vicinity of the Tor should be accompanied by a responsible member of the party. Apart from being a hindrance to rock climbers, there is the obvious danger of a fall resulting from carelessness.

Stanton Moor (G.R. 2463)   An important burial and ceremonial site during the Bronze Age, the little moor once had as many as seventy barrows (burial chambers), all so thoroughly excavated that it is difficult to locate them. However, the Nine Ladies Stone Circle remains as it was, that is apart from the addition of a relatively modern but disintegrating stone wall that encircles it. If approached from the west, locating the circle with neither map nor instructions can make for an interesting half hour, since it is well hidden within a copse. Old quarry workings, woods, a tower and a weathered pinnacle of gritstone with steps cut in (The Cork Stone) add further interest to a rather haunting place.

Rowter Rocks, Birchover (G.R. 235622)   Located behind the Druid Inn at Birchover, it is a gritstone out-crop with man-made tunnels and other weird, sculpted features, their origin being somewhat of a mystery. It is a fascinating place for young and old alike. A visit to Stanton Moor, the inn and the rocks, in any order, makes for an interesting day out.

Bradford Dale, Youlgreave (G.R. 2063) (See Route 10) An ideal location for a picnic, where the river bank is wide and grassy and where the little ones can safely paddle and play. Rope swings, usually *in situ*, provide entertainment for older children. When bored with this, a walk up the dale towards Middleton is both pleasant and interesting, with weirs and fishpools where trout are easily spotted, mixed woodland harbouring all manner of birdlife, and old mine workings to investigate. Near the first footbridge is a little cafe with tea garden overlooking the dale and complementary to its setting.

Rainster Rocks, NW. of Brassington (G.R. 220548) Not really suitable for younger children, the rocks rise in tiers of dolomitic limestone which provide a natural location for exploring and scrambling. However, a wary eye should be kept on the more adventurous child since the tiers are small cliffs only to be approached by the party equipped for rock climbing.

Monsal Dale (G.R. 1771) (See Route 15) Best approached from the White Lodge Picnic Area 2 miles west of Ashford-in-the-Water, the dale is a popular spot for picnickers, paddlers and sunbathers (in season). The riverside is flat and grassy for a mile or so with clumps of trees here and there, the whole picture being more akin to an area of wild parkland rather than wild countryside. On sunny weekends in summer, the area by the weir is a mini coastal resort and best avoided.

Hob's House (G.R. 176714) (See Route 15) Accessible from Monsal Head and described fully in the description for the Monsal Dale walk, it is a delightful place to explore and can be combined with a riverside stop to fill in a whole afternoon.

Chee Dale (G.R. 126735) (See Route 11) The dale can be reached from either Wormhill or Millersdale. A little upstream from the footbridge mentioned in the variation walk, and just before the beginning of the gorge around Chee Tor, the river bank provides a suitable spot for a picnic and a paddle. Though not recommended for younger children, older and more agile youngsters can take a short excursion into the gorge to see its huge cliffs, a justly popular venue for rock climbers, or to sample the stepping stones.

Peter's Stone (G.R. 176754) (See Route 14) Described fully in the description for the Cressbrook Dale walk, it offers considerable attraction to children, with rocks to climb, secret holes and a cave to explore, and fossils to find. The best approach is from Wardlow Mires, as in the above mentioned route description.

COUNTRY PARKS

Alton Towers near Ashbourne. Leisure Park and Gardens, open April to October. Tel. Oakamoor 702458/702449.

Buxton Country Park Woodland walks and interpretation centre. Tel. Buxton 6978.

Chatsworth Farmyard and Adventure Playground. The farm is designed with children in mind, and the adventure playground is superbly constructed. Open Easter to October. Tel. Baslow 2242.

Gulliver's Kingdom, Matlock Bath. Model Village and adventure playground. Open daily. Tel. Matlock 55970.

Riber Castle Wildlife Park near Matlock. British and European birds and animals, vintage car and motorcycle collection, children's playground and model railway. Tel. Matlock 2073.

Lyme Park National Trust Country Park, Disley. A deer park centred on Lyme Hall, with adventure playground.

WET WEATHER ALTERNATIVES Completely or partly under cover.

Caverns and Mines

Bagshaw Cavern, Bradwell. Limestone show cave, open daily, but by appointment only from October to Easter. Tel. Hope Valley 20540.

Blue John Cavern, Castleton. Limestone show cave, open daily all year. Tel. Hope Valley 20638.

Good Luck Mine, Via Gellia, near Cromford. A working example of a mid-eighteenth century lead mine. Open on first Sunday of each month, or by appointment. Tel. Chesterfield 72375.

Great Masson Cavern, Heights of Abraham, Matlock Bath. Limestone show cave, open Sundays and Bank Holidays from Easter to October and daily during August. Tel. Matlock 2365.

Great Rutland Cavern and Nestus Mine, Heights of Abraham, Matlock Bath. Limestone show cave, within which is a 17th century lead mine. Open daily from Easter to October. Tel. Matlock 2365.

Holme Bank Chert Mine, Bakewell, Limestone show cave, open Easter to October. Tel. Darley Dale 4658.

Peak Cavern, Castleton. Limestone show cave, open April to September. Tel. Hope Valley 20285.

Poole's Cavern, Buxton Country Park. Limestone show cave, open Easter to October. Tel. Buxton 6978.

Speedwell Cavern, Castleton. Limestone cave with underground boat ride, open daily all year. Tel. Hope Valley 20512.

Temple Mine, Matlock Bath, Fluorite and lead mine, open daily all year. Tel. Matlock 3834.

Treak Cliff Cavern, Castleton. Limestone show cave with fine grottoes, and veins of Blue John stone. Open daily all year. Tel. Hope Valley 20571.

MUSEUMS, HOUSES AND INDUSTRIAL ARCHAEOLOGY

Aquarium and Waxworks Museum, Matlock Bath. Tel. Matlock 3624.

Buxton Micrarium. Nature seen through microscopes. Open April to November. Tel. Buxton 78662.

Buxton Museum. Archaeological relics of the Peak District. Closed on Mondays. Tel. Buxton 4658.

Caudwell's Mill, Rowsley. A working, water-power, roller flour mill. Open Easter to October. Tel. Matlock 734374.

Cavendish House Museum, Castleton. Houses the Ollernshaw Collection of Blue John, etc. Open daily all year. Tel. Hope Valley 20642.

Chatsworth House. Home of the Duke of Devonshire, open April to October. Tel. Baslow 2242.

Crich Tramway Museum. Turn off A6 at Whatstandwell or off A610 at Bullbridge. Tram rides, period street etc. Open April to October. Tel. Ambergate 2565.

Cromford Canal Wharf. Canal trips by horse-drawn boat. Tel. Wirksworth 3921.

Haddon Hall, near Bakewell. The Duke of Rutland's Medieval Hall. Open Tuesdays to Saturdays, April to September. Tel. Bakewell 2855.

Longnor Folk Museum. Exhibits and spinning demonstrations. Open Saturdays and Bank Holidays from Spring Bank Holiday week-end to end of first week in September, 2.30 - 4.30.

Magpie Mine, Sheldon. Remains of lead mine including chimneys, engine house and winding gear. Information about access from Peak District Mining Museum, Matlock Bath. Tel. Matlock 3834.

Middleton Top Engine House. Winding engine of former Cromford and High Peak Railway. Open Sundays and first Saturday of each month, when the engine is in steam. Tel. Wirksworth 3204.

Old House Museum, Bakewell. Tudor house and Folk Museum. Open daily, Easter to October. Tel. Bakewell 3647.

Peak District Mining Museum, Matlock Bath. Exhibits and displays illustrating 2000 years of lead mining. Climbing shaft between floors for children. Open daily all year. Tel. Matlock 3834.

Peak Rail, Buxton. Steam rides, April to September at week-ends and Bank Holidays. Tel. Buxton 77763.

Peveril Castle, Castleton. Impressive ruined Norman castle with keep. Splendid views over Castleton and surrounding countryside. Open daily all year. Tel. Hope Valley 20613.

SWIMMING POOLS

There are indoor pools at Ashbourne, Buxton, Leek and Matlock.

All the information given here was correct on publication, but times of opening etc. are sometimes altered at short notice, so do please check before setting off on a grand expedition!

PUBS AND INNS CATERING FOR FAMILIES

Below is a list of some of the village pubs and inns in the area covered by this guide, the licensees of which make provision for families with young children. To locate them, refer to the map at the beginning of the guide.

Alstonefield — George Inn.

Ashford-in-the-Water — Bull's Head and Devonshire Arms.

Bakewell — Manners Hotel and Peacock.

Beeley — (4 miles south of Baslow on B6012) Devonshire Arms.

Biggin — Waterloo Inn.

Butterton — Black Lion Inn.

Dovedale — (halfway between Thorpe and Ilam) Izaak Walton Hotel.

Grindon — Cavalier Inn.

Gt. Longstone — White Lion

Hartington — Charles Cotton Hotel and Devonshire Arms☆ (Large children's room with various games).

Litton — Red Lion.

Longnor — Crewe and Harpur Arms.

Millersdale — Angler's Rest.

Monsal Head — (1½ miles north west of Ashford on B6465) Monsal Head Hotel.

Over Haddon — (2 miles south west of Bakewell off B5055) Lathkill Hotel.

Parwich — (5 miles north of Ashbourne between B5056 and A515) Sycamore Inn.

Stoney Middleton — Royal Oak.

Tideswell — George Hotel and Horse and Jockey.

Wardlow Mires — Three Stags' Head.

Youlgreave — Bull's Head, Farmer's Arms & George Hotel.

FAMILY WALKS SERIES

Family Walks in the Lake District. Barry McKay. ISBN 0 907758 40 1.

Family Walks in West Yorkshire. Howard Beck. ISBN 0 907758 43 6.

Family Walks in Three Peaks and Malham. Howard Beck. ISBN 0 907758 42 8.

Family Walks in South Yorkshire. Norman Taylor. ISBN 0 907758 25 8.

Family Walks in Cheshire. Chris Buckland. ISBN 0 907758 29 0.

Family Walks in the Staffordshire Peak and Potteries. Les Lumsdon. ISBN 0 907758 34 7.

Family Walks in the White Peak. Norman Taylor. ISBN 0 907758 09 6.

Family Walks in the Dark Peak. Norman Taylor. ISBN 0 907758 16 9.

Family Walks in Snowdonia. Laurence Main. ISBN 0 907758 32 0.

Family Walks in Mid Wales. Laurence Main. ISBN 0 907758 27 4.

Family Walks in South Shropshire. Marian Newton. ISBN 0 907758 30 4.

Family Walks in the Teme Valley. Camilla Harrison. ISBN 0 907758 45 2.

Family Walks in Hereford and Worcester. Gordon Ottewell. ISBN 0 907758 20 7.

Family Walks in the Wye Valley. Heather and Jon Hurley. ISBN 0 907758 26 6.

Family Walks in the Cotswolds. Gordon Ottewell. ISBN 0 907758 15 0.

Family Walks in South Gloucestershire. Gordon Ottewell. ISBN 0 907758 33 9.

Family Walks in Oxfordshire. Laurence Main. ISBN 0 907758 38 X.

Family Walks around Bristol, Bath and the Mendips. Nigel Vile. ISBN 0 907758 19 3.

Family Walks in Wiltshire. Nigel Vile. ISBN 0 907758 21 5.

Family Walks in Berkshire and North Hampshire. Kathy Sharp. ISBN 0 907758 37 1.

Family Walks on Exmoor and the Quantocks John Caswell. ISBN 0 907758 46 0.

Family Walks in Mendip, Avalon and Sedgemoor. Nigel Vile. ISBN 0 907758 41 X.

Family Walks in North West Kent. Clive Cutter. ISBN 0 907758 36 3.

Ready Spring 1992

Family Walks in the Weald of Kent and Sussex
Family Walks in North Yorkshire
Family Walks around Luton and Dunstable
Family Walks in Northumbria   Other titles under consideration
Family Walks in Nottinghamshire
Family Walks on the Isle of Wight
Family Walks in Clwyd
Family Walks in Dorset
Family Walks in Rossendale, Pendle and Bowland

The Publishers, D. J. Mitchell and E. G. Power welcome suggestions for further titles in this Series; and will be pleased to consider other manuscripts of Derbyshire and regional interest from new or established authors.

Scarthin Books of Cromford are the leading Peak District specialists in secondhand and antiquarian books, and purchase good books, music, maps and photographs at fair and informed valuations.
Contact Dr. D. J. Mitchell by letter, or phone Matlock (0629) 823272.